THE
SHARK
WATCHERS'
GUIDE

To Dr. Gilman,

With best wishes,

Yours sincerely

THE SHARK WATCHERS' GUIDE

Guido Dingerkus

Illustrated by Dietrich Bürkel

Preface by Eugenie Clark

Wanderer Books
Published by Simon & Schuster, Inc., New York

Published by WANDERER BOOKS
A Division of Simon & Schuster, Inc.
Simon & Schuster Building
1230 Avenue of the Americas
New York, New York 10020
WANDERER and colophon are registered
trademarks of Simon & Schuster, Inc.
Also available in JULIAN MESSNER Library Edition
Designed by Teresa Delgado, A Good Thing, Inc.
Manufactured in the United States of America
10 9 8 7 6 5 4 3 2 1

Library of Congress Cataloging in Publication Data
Dingerkus, Guido.
    The shark watchers' guide.

    Bibliography: p.
    Includes index
    Summary: Describes the characteristics, habits,
and natural environment of various species of sharks
and discusses their relationship to human beings.
    1. Sharks [1. Sharks] I. Bürkel, Dietrich, ill.
II. Title
QL638.9.D56   1985   597'.31   84-22648
ISBN: 0-671-50234-4 (Lib. bdg.)
ISBN: 0-671-55038-1 Pbk.

Contents

Preface

There is an evolution taking place in our attitude towards sharks. A few years ago, the fear of sharks reached a peak with the "Jawsmania" created by writers and film producers. Using the shark as a horror star for an audience who knew the marine worlds of William Beebe, Rachel Carson and Jacques Cousteau, Hollywood put a Frankenstein monster or Dracula underwater. Many people in the audience could identify with the situation.

Not many people understand what a shark is really like, but, after *Jaws*, they began to wonder. The fisherman who accidentally catches a small shark on his line is no longer satisfied to have it identified as a "sand shark"—that catchall term that can include a dozen different species of sharks. People interested in the sea want more information about its creatures. We have become acutely aware of pollution problems, the loss or ugly transformation of some of our beautiful coastal sea areas, and the threatened extinction of some wonderful sea creatures.

President Reagan proclaimed July 1984 to June 1985 as the YEAR OF THE OCEAN—a time for all of us to focus our efforts on understanding the sea and its creatures and how we might more wisely use our relationship with this environment. As one of the most magnificent animals in the sea, the shark deserves its full share of understanding.

I believe the time has come to love and enjoy sharks as well as make an effort to understand them and utilize them more wisely. These beautiful and unique fish, which make up more than 300 species, benefit people in many ways. They are subjects of study in medical research and parts of sharks are used in medicine and surgery, health foods, and cosmetics.

For sheer enjoyment and fascination, watch sharks through the glass of giant aquariums.

If you are a diver, for the ultimate thrill and pleasure, observe sharks near a coral reef (but be careful to avoid any sudden movement or you may scare them away before you get their picture). In the past few years, hundreds of divers have experienced the *safety* of diving with schools of large scalloped hammerhead sharks. On three trips to the Sea of Cortez at the sea mounts near La Paz, Mexico, I've shared this unique and wonderful sight with over 40 divers, many of whom had never seen a shark before. Even the most timid and apprehensive diver, after a first experience could hardly wait to dive with the hammerheads again.

Try eating sharks, if you haven't already. They are a delicious, wholesome food without bones.

Wear sharks—they make beautiful and strong leather belts, boots, and bags. Their skin is cleverly processed in Japan where almost every part of a shark's body is utilized. The muscles of millions of sharks are eaten by people every year. It would be frugal to use the other parts as well.

It's time to stop fearing sharks; neglecting to buckle the seat belt while riding in your car is many times more dangerous than meeting a shark. Watch the educational and, yes, also the fun films on TV and at the movies. Good ichthyological science fiction like *Jaws* satisfies that search for thrills that we all possess, but don't take the shark horror films any more seriously than Frankenstein's monster or Count Dracula.

It's time to respect sharks and get to know more about them. Scientists have increased our knowledge about the biology and ecology of sharks in the last two decades. Sharks are not the stupid, unpredictable creatures we once thought them to be.

We should continue to learn about sharks and be fair to them. We still know little about their populations and how much we will threaten the extinction of some species if we keep fishing in unlimited quantities. Man is more the predator of sharks than vice versa. One has only to see the tons of sharks sold each day at the Tokyo fish market to be convinced of this.

Learn more about sharks, what they are really like, how they live and reproduce. Nothing could be more fascinating. And even learn to love them as pets.

Guido Dingerkus will tell you how.

Eugenie Clark
October, 1984

What Is a Shark?

The word "shark" strikes fear into the hearts of many people. Recently their fear has been intensified by books and movies like *Jaws*. They believe sharks to be large, menacing monsters lurking near every beach, waiting for people to go swimming so that the sharks can attack and eat them.

The truth is very different. All sharks are predators; none of them eat plants. They pursue and capture their food, but their diets vary greatly from group to group. Some sharks eat crabs and clams from the ocean floor. Others feed exclusively on fish or marine mammals, and some—especially the giants such as the whale shark and basking shark—are filter feeders that eat only microscopic animals. Of the great number of species of sharks, only six are known to attack humans.

The great white shark has given its bad reputation as a dreaded killer to all sharks. The great white is an awe-inspiring sight, twisting and thrusting through the water, impelled by its powerful fins. Its torpedo-shaped body allows it to move through the water swiftly and smoothly.

Although the mako shark can attain speeds up to 50 mph, most sharks swim at only 20 to 30 mph. They will use their fastest speed when they are attacking their prey. Depending on the species, the prey might be crabs, clams, fish, seals, porpoises, sea turtles, or even whales. Some kinds of sharks will eat their prey whole; others will bite circular chunks out of their prey with their razor-sharp teeth.

Sharks are often referred to as "perfect killing machines," and if you saw a shark attack its prey you would see how these creatures earned this description. From a distance, a shark can smell its prey, or can feel the pressure waves produced by the prey's movements in water. When close enough to the prey, the shark homes in by vision. It may circle the prey a few times, watching it closely, but once it decides to attack, a few swift strong thrusts of its tail fin will drive the shark toward its prey with incredible force. Closing its eyes during the last moments of the attack to prevent the prey from injuring its eyes during the death struggle, for the last few feet the shark relies on the prey's own body electricity for target signals to home in on.

As the shark grabs the prey, its jaws actually dislocate and protrude out of the shark's mouth. Strong jaw muscles then close the razor-sharp teeth on the prey with such force that they bite through skin, flesh, cartilage, and bone like a knife through butter. With a few sideways shakes of its head, the shark removes a circular piece of flesh that looks as if it had been cut out by a surgeon.

Sharks come in all shapes and sizes, and they live differently from one another. Some have beautiful skin colors and patterns. Sharks are graceful in the water. Most are sleek and elegant swimmers with streamlined bodies that allow them to move through the water seemingly without effort.

Sharks are useful scavengers in the sea, feeding on carcasses and other debris in the water. Like wolves, which were also long maligned, sharks feed on sick, old, and dying creatures, and so they play an important ecological role in their environment.

Worldwide there are about three hundred species of sharks in about twenty-five families. They are found in all oceans and at all depths. Some species, like the Greenland shark, live mainly in cold Arctic waters; and other forms, like the Portuguese shark and the recently discovered megamouth shark, live only in the greatest depths of the oceans. The nurse shark lives on the bottom, but in quite shallow water, but most sharks live in temperate and tropical waters at or near the surface.

Some sharks, like the zebra, carpet, and leopard sharks, have beautifully colored and patterned skin. In size, sharks range from the dwarf shark, which is 6 inches long as a full-grown adult, to the giant 60-foot whale shark. The whale shark, despite its size, is totally harmless as it is a filter feeder, eat-

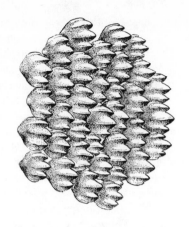

Typical Requiem Shark (Carcharhinid)

Typical Catshark (Scyliorhinid)

towards
Head

towards
Tail

Close-up of dermal denticles

ing only microscopic animals. Of course, if provoked, all sharks can bite, just as a pet dog or cat can.

Fishes in general are divided into two groups: the jawless fishes such as lampreys and hagfishes, and the jawed fishes. Among the jawed fishes, sharks are in the class *Chondrichthyes.* This name comes from the Greek words *chondros,* meaning cartilage, and *ichthyos,* meaning fish; they are the "cartilage fishes." There is not a single bone in the shark's entire body, just cartilage. Also in this group are ratfish or rabbitfish, skates, and rays.

The other group of jawed fishes are the bony ones we are all familiar with, like the salmon or trout.

How do we know a shark is a shark? This sounds like a simple question, but some sharks do not look at all like what most people think of as typical sharks. Scientists look for two distinguishing features. Sharks along with skates and rays, which are really just flattened sharks, can be distinguished by their five to seven pairs of gill openings. In addition their skin, instead of being covered with scales, is covered by dermal denticles—which are small skin teeth. If you run your hand over a shark's skin going with the dermal denticles, it will feel quite smooth. However, if you rub your hand backwards over the skin, your hand will be severely cut by the razor-sharp edges of the dermal denticles.

Basically, all sharks have streamlined, torpedo-shaped bodies that allow them to move through the water easily and rapidly. The shark's body is ideal for a fast-swimming sea predator, perfectly adapted to the shark's predatory life.

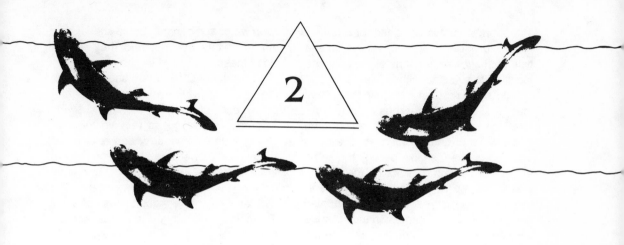

A Shark's Body—
Form and Function

A shark's body is designed for one purpose—to obtain food. Depending on the type of shark, various parts of the body are modified to suit its particular way of life.

Before sharks can eat their food, they must first find it. Numerous sensory features aid them in finding food, giving them many ways of finding out what is around them. In the sea, sharks occupy the same ecological position as lions on the African plains: the top of the food pyramid. Only two creatures are the shark's enemy: human beings and larger sharks. Sharks' senses allowed them to attain their position in the oceans, and to maintain it for millions of years. They use their eyes and nostrils much as we do, to see and to smell. However, a shark *only* smells with its nostrils: it does not breathe through them.

Contrary to what most people believe, sharks have rather good vision. Depending on water clarity, they can see up to 100 feet. In the back wall of their eyes is a special set of cells that act as mirrors, amplifying the light so that sharks can see in deep water and at night. Some sharks have opaque white eyelids, and they always close these eyelids when they bite.

Dr. Eugenie Clark, while she was working at the Cape Haze Marine Laboratory, did experiments in which she trained sharks to come to a target to receive food. By changing the shape, size, and color of this target, she learned that sharks can discriminate between shapes, sizes, and even colors.

Sharks have a very good sense of smell. The portion of a shark's brain that controls smell is very large—twice as large as the rest of the brain. A shark can detect one part of blood in 100 million parts of water. That's like being able to smell one drop of blood in 25 gallons of water. With such a keen sense of smell, is it any wonder that sharks have been called the hounds of the sea? Scientists have done experiments in tanks to see what chemicals, at what levels, are stimulating to sharks. These experiments have shown that body fluids, especially blood, are most stimulating. In

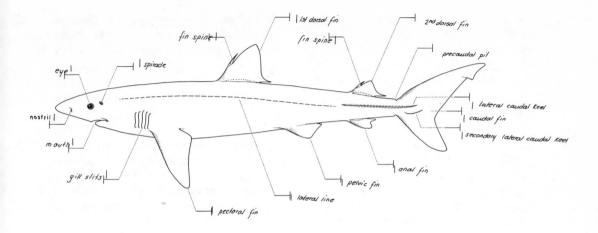

the open ocean, sharks have been observed to follow chum slicks (made up of ground up fish) for several miles to their source.

Sharks, like most other fishes, have a lateral line system along the side of the body. The lateral line is a series of fluid-filled canals. These canals are attached to nerves that are very sensitive to waves—whether they are sound waves or pressure waves. Thus, a shark can "hear" through these canals, and it can also "feel" other fish and animals passing it by means of the pressure waves these creatures produce in the water surrounding the shark—much like the bow waves of a ship. With this lateral line a shark can "hear" sounds or detect vibrations that are over 600 feet away. On the

17

head of a shark are modified portions of the lateral lines, called the *ampullae of Lorenzini.*

The ampullae of Lorenzini are a fine, netlike extension of the lateral line. Unlike the rest of the lateral line, these canals are electroreceptors. The shark's ampullae of Lorenzini are the most sensitive electroreceptors known among animals; they can detect as little as one-millionth of a volt. All animals produce minute amounts of electricity, mainly from their nerves. Sharks can locate and catch food animals just by perceiving the electricity their prey emit. In laboratory tests sharks did not attack animals that had their body electricity insulated from the sharks, but they aggressively attacked mechanical generators that mimicked the electrical output of a prey's body.

Possibly associated with the ampullae of Lorenzini is the shark's compass sense. Recent studies have shown that sharks can detect geomagnetic fields produced by the earth. Utilizing these fields and its compass sense—just as a person would use a compass—a shark can orient itself, navigate, and home in on a given location. This may help explain how sharks return to the same feeding, breeding, and pupping areas every year.

Unlike human beings, who have taste buds only on their tongues, sharks have taste buds in their throat, on their tongue, and all through their mouth. Sharks that have barbels—threadlike growths on their lips—like the nurse shark, also have taste buds on these barbels. The shark's sense of taste is very acute, and some species of sharks have very definite likes and dislikes. Recent experiments have shown that sea hares, *Aplysia,* are very distasteful to sharks, which will immediately reject any object that has been in contact with a sea hare. Sharks definitely prefer the taste of certain creatures, such as tunas and sea turtles.

Once a shark has located its food, it must pursue and attack it. The shark's streamlined, torpedo-shaped body allows it to outswim its prey.

Most people recognize a shark by the large, conspicuous, triangular dorsal fin on its back. However, this is only one of the many fins that give the shark thrust for swimming and control of the direction in which it moves.

A shark's fins can be unpaired or paired. Unpaired fins can have three locations on sharks: *dorsal* (on the back), *anal* (beneath), or *caudal* (the tail itself). Because it is located in the middle of the back, the dorsal fin is also called a median fin. Some sharks have two dorsal fins, one behind the other; some have only one. Most sharks have one large dorsal fin on the back, and a second—often much smaller—one on top of the tail. Spiny dogfish sharks and horn sharks have two dorsal fins, each preceded by a large spine. An anal fin, underneath the tail, is present in some but not all sharks.

The caudal fin, or tail fin, which gives the main forward swimming thrust to the fish, varies greatly in shape. In most sharks the caudal fin is asymmetrical, the top half being much larger than the bottom half. An extreme example is the caudal fin of the thresher shark. In other sharks, such as the great white shark, the top and bottom halves of the caudal fin are the same size, so the fin is symmetrical. The caudal fin of a shark gives it propulsion by regular, wavy side-to-side movements.

Sharks have two sets of paired fins—the *pectoral fins* in the front and the *pelvic fins* in the middle. In most species the front fins are rigid but can be moved up and down slightly to act as steering rudders, helping to guide the fish up and down or right and left. Also in some species they are used in behavioral displays, such as the reef shark's threat display. In male sharks, the pelvic fins are modified into *claspers,* which the male uses during mating.

Many of the faster-swimming sharks also have keels. These are enlarged lateral ridges on the side of the tail that help give speed and maneuverability to a shark.

Since a shark's skeleton is made of cartilage, its body is flexible. This, combined with its fins, gives sharks maneuverability; they can actually turn completely around within the length of their body.

With the thrust produced by their tail,

sharks are among the fastest swimmers in the sea, reaching 30 and 40 mph for short bursts.

The brain, as in all animals, regulates the shark's entire body and all of its movements. The brain is encased in the cartilaginous skull and is rather small, simple, and primitive. Because the brain is so small and primitive, many of the shark's actions are based on instinct rather than thought. However, Dr. Eugenie Clark, while she was at the Cape Haze Marine Laboratory, found that sharks could be trained to come to a target and be rewarded with food in response to a command, such as the ringing of a bell. They were also able to remember this for a period of time, so they do have some ability to remember things. However,

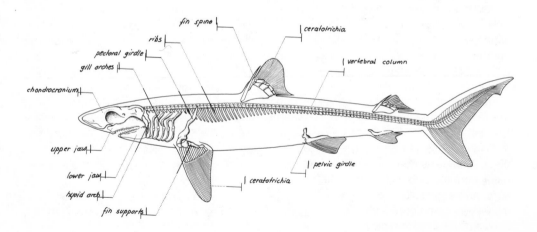

it does not appear that they can learn the more complicated tricks that seals and porpoises can do.

Most of the brain of a shark serves to receive sensory input. As mentioned earlier, the olfactory bulbs for smell make up over half the size of the brain. The optic bulbs, for vision, are also quite large. The cerebrum, which is very large (over half the entire brain) in human beings and is used for memory and thinking, is very small in sharks. The cerebellum, which controls coordination and reflexes, is about one-quarter the total brain size in sharks and is responsible for much of their instinctive behavior.

From the brain the spinal cord runs down the shark's back in the vertebral column. Emerging from the spinal cord are most of the nerves that run throughout the shark's body. A small number of nerves emerge directly from the brain. The nerves carry sensory messages to the brain and bring messages from the brain to the rest of the body, telling it what to do.

Once a shark has located its food it must pursue and grab hold of it. That is where the jaws and teeth (the most feared parts of a shark) come into play.

Sharks' teeth are not imbedded in the jaws, like human teeth. Instead, they are set in gums that rest on the jaws. Sharks are constantly replacing their teeth They have from five to twenty rows of them, and the youngest teeth make up the back row. In most species the teeth are broad, thin, and daggerlike, with razor-sharp edges. Sharks ordinarily use only the front row to grasp and chew their food. As these teeth fall out or are worn out, the next row moves forward to become the functioning teeth, almost as in a conveyor-belt system. Thus, sharks always have many reserve teeth. When a shark is growing, it may replace its front row of teeth every seven days; in ten years a shark may go through twenty thousand teeth.

This may help explain why fossil shark teeth are so common whereas whole skeletons are so rare. Most of the fossils are

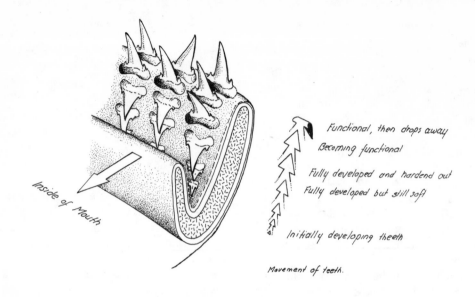

Inside of Mouth

Functional, then drops away

Becoming functional

Fully developed and hardened out

Fully developed but still soft

Initially developing teeth

Movement of teeth.

probably shed teeth. Some sharks have up to three thousand teeth in their jaws at any one time.

When a shark bites, it can exert a force of up to 44,000 pounds per square inch. In comparison, a human bite creates a pressure of only about 150 pounds per square inch. With its large numbers of razor-sharp teeth and its powerful jaws, a shark can easily bite through flesh and bones.

Sharks cannot move their jaws from side to side; hence they cannot chew their food, as we do. Instead they swallow it whole, if it is small enough. If it's large, they grab hold of the prey with their jaws and shake their heads from side to side to saw off a chunk with their teeth. Then they swallow the chunk whole.

The food then enters the esophagus at the rear of the mouth and passes down into the stomach, where digestion begins. The digestive juices in a shark's stomach are so strong they will corrode stainless steel. Hence almost anything a shark takes into

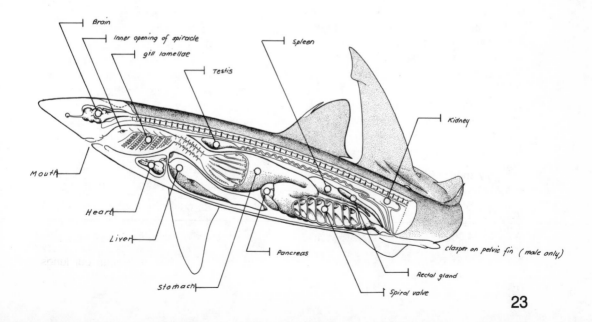

Brain

Inner opening of spiracle

gill lamellae

Testis

Spleen

Kidney

Mouth

Heart

Liver

Pancreas

clasper on pelvic fin (male only)

Rectal gland

Stomach

Spiral valve

its stomach will be digested, including skin, hair, bone, and cartilage. This may help explain why many sharks are not selective feeders; shoes, license plates, cans of paint, and rolls of tar paper have been found in their stomachs.

Food then passes into the intestines, where it is absorbed. Sharks have a *spiral valve*—a device shaped like a spiral staircase—inside their intestines. This increases the capacity of the intestines and allows them to absorb the food better. Wastes that are not digestible then leave the body through the *cloaca.* Near the cloaca is a small rectal gland that aids in maintaining the shark's salt balance. A gall bladder produces digestive juices called *bile,* which pass into the stomach to help digestion. The pancreas also produces digestive enzymes.

The liver, which is at the front end of the abdominal cavity, is very large. Sharks do not have any fat; food reserves are stored as oil, mainly in the shark's liver. Remember that oil is buoyant—it floats on water.

Sharks do not have air bladders, like most bony fishes, nor do they have lungs or other air chambers in their body as human beings do. When we go into the water, we rely on the air in our lungs to help us float. The oil in a shark's liver is what helps make it buoyant, and there is plenty of it. A 15-foot tiger shark's liver can contain 18 gallons of oil. Without this oil, the shark would just sink to the ocean floor and stay there.

The heart lies in a chamber behind the gills, below the esophagus and in front of the liver. A shark's heart has only two chambers—as opposed to the four chambers of a mammal's heart—and thus is considered rather primitive. The heart pumps blood, which is produced in the spleen, throughout the entire shark's body by means of a system of arteries and veins.

The blood gets nutrients from the digested food in the intestines and carries them to all cells of the body. The blood also picks up oxygen absorbed by the gills and takes it to all cells of the body. Just as we need the air we take in through our lungs to supply oxygen to all our body's cells, a shark's body cells need oxygen to survive. The shark's blood also carries waste products to the kidneys. There the waste products are removed from the blood and then excreted as urine.

As mentioned earlier, sharks use their nostrils only for smelling, not for breathing. Instead, they take in water, which contains oxygen, through the mouth. Many sharks have a *spiracle* that aids in bringing water in through the gills, also. The spiracle is a short tube that opens to the outside behind the eyes, and internally carries the oxygenated water to the gills, where the oxygen is absorbed.

Just behind the head are the gills. They remove oxygen from the water and take it into the body—the shark's way of breathing. There are five to seven pairs of gills in a shark, depending on the species. Each gill has its own opening to the outside, through which water goes out after having passed over the gills. On the gills are *lamellae*—fingerlike projections—that are filled with tiny blood vessels called *capillaries*. Through the capillaries and the very thin skin of the lamellae, the blood absorbs the oxygen from the water passing through the gills.

The cartilage that makes up the shark's skeleton often incorporates crystals of calcium. These harden and strengthen the cartilage and makes it look and feel almost as hard as bone.

A shark's skull, which is also called the *chondrocranium,* is one piece of this cartilaginous skeleton. The skulls of other fish and vertebrates are made up of several chunks. The upper and lower jaws of the shark are both made up of two segments— one on the right and another on the left—to which the shark's teeth are attached. The jaws are only loosely attached to the skull, thus allowing for the movement of the jaws. When feeding, a shark can throw its jaws a fair distance out and forward to help it grasp food.

Directly behind the jaws is a series of *gill arches.* These support the gills, used for breathing. Most shark species have five sets of gill arches, but a few, among them the frilled shark, have six or seven gill arches.

Behind, and attached to, the rear of the chondrocranium are the *vertebral centra,* which run down the entire length of the shark's back. They serve to support its body and encase and protect the spinal cord. Projecting outward from the most anterior (forward) centra are several short ribs.

The shark's fins are supported by cartilage. The inner portion of each fin consists of large *basal elements* and *radials,* and the outer portion of the radials has fringe-like cartilage bristles called *ceratotrichia.* The dorsal, caudal, and anal fins' basal elements are attached directly to the vertebral centra. The two pectoral fins are held together by a mass of cartilage called the *pectoral girdle.* Similarly, the pelvic fins are joined together by cartilaginous structures called the *pelvic girdle.*

The kidneys are at the top of the abdominal cavity, just below the vertebral column, and are dark red. Directly below the kidneys are the reproductive organs—testes in the male and ovaries in the female. These are usually whitish and are fairly small, but when the ovaries are producing eggs are usually yellow like the yolk of a hen's egg but in some species they are a paler color.

Female sharks give birth to their young in one of three ways. *Oviparous* sharks lay eggs; *ovoviviparous* sharks retain the eggs inside their bodies until the young are ready to hatch; and in the rest—the *viviparous* sharks—the young are born alive and there exists a connection much like a placenta between the female and her young. Sharks, unlike most other fishes, have internal fertilization. In order to accomplish this, the male shark uses its two claspers—specially modified parts of its pelvic fins—to introduce sperm into the female. During mating the male shark grasps the female's fins or back with his mouth and then wraps his body around the female. Because of this most adult female sharks have heavily scarred backs. During the mating time the male does not feed—a mechanism designed by nature presumably to keep the male from eating the female during this courtship period.

The eggs of nurse sharks, horn sharks, whale sharks, and cat sharks have a tough, leathery "shell" around them. Most sharks lay their eggs on the ocean bottom, where they are attached to rocks or seaweed by long stringlike tendrils. Horn sharks, however, lay unique screw-shaped egg cases. The female shark picks up these eggs in her mouth and literally screws them into cracks between rocks and sunken pieces of wood. Depending on the species of shark, the eggs hatch in six to fifteen months.

Among sharks that bear their young alive, the developing baby sharks, or pups, inside the female either live off their eggs' yolk or get nourishment directly from the female's bloodstream. The young may stay inside the mother for up to two years. In one species of shark, at least, the young are cannibalistic before they are born. Inside female sand tiger sharks, the pups will devour one another until only two are left—one in the female's right uterus, and one in the left uterus. The number of baby sharks born at one time varies from two to a hundred, depending on the species of shark.

When the female is ready to give birth to her young she goes to a pupping ground—usually a shallow bay or estuary—where she will congregate with other females who are pupping. During this time the females do not feed—a mechanism that prevents them from eating their own young. The females leave the pupping ground soon after giving birth, but the young will stay in the area until they are old enough to fend for themselves in the open ocean where larger sharks, including their parents, are waiting to devour them. Few will reach maturity, which in most species is ten to fifteen years.

In most species pupping takes place in the spring and is soon followed by another breeding, to start another generation of sharks.

Places to See Sharks

Good places to see sharks are the spots where people go fishing in salt water. People who are bottom-fishing for flounder, fluke, and other bottom-dwelling bony fishes sometimes catch smooth dogfish sharks, horn sharks, or angel sharks. These sharks, like the bottom-dwelling bony fish, feed on crabs, clams, shrimp, and squid.

Many fishermen try to catch the larger sharks, especially the great white sharks and mako sharks, several miles offshore. They lure these sharks to the baited hook by using ground up fish or meat, called chum, which is usually soupy. The fishermen ladle the chum into the water a cup at a time. It forms a thin layer on the surface, called a slick. The chum slick then slowly floats away from the boat. A shark encountering this chum slick will become excited by it and follow it to the boat. Shark fishers must use a strong pole and heavy fishing line, and they need great strength and endurance. A several-hundred-pound shark will give a tremendous fight once hooked. Some sharks have struggled more than ten hours before being landed. Many sharks are classified as game fishes, and great white sharks and mako sharks will make spectacular leaps into the air after being hooked, much like salmon or trout.

Shark tournaments and commercial fishing can severely reduce the number of sharks. Since many species do not mature until they are fifteen to twenty years old, and because they produce a fairly small number of young every year, shark populations are very sensitive to fishing. Indeed, as with the great whales, fishing can quickly lead to danger of extinction. Mackerel sharks, for example, were once quite common off the New England coast. Several years of intense commercial fishing, however, have reduced their populations to the point where they are now rare, perhaps even extinct, in this area.

Diving is an excellent way to see sharks, but it can be extremely dangerous if not done with caution. Never dive in an area where there are sharks without getting advice from a professional diver or shark expert. Remember one thing above all: Never molest or antagonize a shark. Any animal

SHARK FACTS AND FIGURES

	Species	Comments
Largest	Whale shark	Commonly reaches over 45 feet. A reported 60-foot, 9-inch whale shark, weighing an estimated 90,000 pounds was caught in the Gulf of Siam in 1919.
Smallest	Dwarf shark	Matures at 6 inches total length.
Most common	Spiny dogfish shark	Tens of millions of pounds caught every year in the North Atlantic Ocean alone.
Rarest	Megamouth shark	At present known from only one individual caught off Oahu, Hawaii.
Deepest	Portuguese shark	Caught at a depth of over 9,000 feet (about 1½ miles).
Fastest	Mako shark	Recorded swimming over 60 mph.
Most Dangerous to People	Great white shark	39 recorded unprovoked attacks on humans.
Largest Litter	Blue shark	One female reportedly had 135 pups in her uterus.
Smallest Litter	Sand tiger shark	Produces only two pups at a time, one in each uterus, due to in-uterine cannibalism of the embryos.
Poisonous Flesh	Greenland shark	Only shark known to be poisonous to human beings when eaten.
Poisonous Spines	Spiny dogfish shark	Only shark known to have poisonous spines, painful but not fatal to humans.

will protect itself when attacked. Many divers have been badly injured by nurse sharks, which normally are peaceable and unaggressive. These divers found nurse sharks sitting on the bottom, where they spend most of their time. Then divers grabbed them, thinking it would be fun to wrestle with a shark or hitch a ride on one. The strong sharks quickly overpowered the divers.

Some scientists and other competent divers plan encounters with sharks. They usually lure the sharks in with chum or bait, just as fishermen do. Sharks that can be lured in with food are usually hungry, and often a feeding frenzy will occur. In a feeding frenzy a group of sharks, attracted and stimulated by the sight and smell of food, will become highly excited and try to eat almost anything. Even sharks that normally hunt alone will congregate when attracted by a strong food scent. At such a time divers must be inside a shark cage, for more than a hundred hungry sharks may be attracted to one spot.

In unplanned encounters with sharks, however, you won't have a shark cage at hand. It is impossible to carry one around whenever you dive. When diving or swimming in waters where large predatory sharks are common—mainly in tropical and subtropical waters—you can do several things to make an unplanned shark encounter less hazardous.

Always dive with two or more companions. This way people can look in several directions to spot a shark before it comes in close; normally sharks will circle their prey before they attack. Also, minimize your attractiveness to sharks. Do not dive when you are bleeding or when you have open wounds. These will give off odors that are attractive to sharks. Do not swim or move fast or in jerky movements. To a shark such motions indicate a sick or wounded animal. Use slow, rhythmical movements. If you are spearing fish, do not carry dead or wounded fish; they will attract sharks. Tow the fish on a long line behind you. This way if a shark is attracted by the scent, it will reach the fish before it gets to you, giving you time to escape. You may lose your fish, but you won't lose your life.

If you do sight a shark, remain motionless. Sharks are attracted by movement. If the shark doesn't smell food and isn't attracted by movement, normally it will lose interest in you and swim away. Some sharks are territorial, however, and such a shark may feel you are invading its territory. When this happens, the shark will display a threat behavior. It will arch its back and drop its pectoral fins downward. It will then swim back and forth slowly. If you see a shark do this, swim away as swiftly and smoothly as you can. It normally will not attack if you retreat, but if you do not swim away, it will attack aggressively.

If the shark does approach you and appears to be attacking, the best thing to do is hit it hard on the nose with any object, even your fist. Sharks have very sensitive noses, and they bump other sharks on the nose to tell them not to attack or bite. If you observe sharks in a feeding frenzy, you will notice they never bite one another. That is because they communicate with one another by bumping noses. Hitting a shark on its nose will almost always deter it from biting. Above all, remain calm. If the shark does not attack, you will have an unrivaled experience observing these fantastic creatures in their natural habitat.

Aquariums are excellent places to observe sharks. Many aquariums have large and dramatic shark exhibits, where you can see sharks in natural-looking displays. Some of the aquariums with the finest shark exhibits are Steinhart Aquarium in San Francisco, California; Seaworld in Orlando, Florida, and San Diego, California; Miami Seaquarium in Miami, Florida; Shedd Aquarium in Chicago, Illinois; the New England Aquarium in Boston, Massachusetts; the Baltimore Aquarium in Baltimore, Maryland; and the New York Aquarium in Coney Island, New York City.

When you go to one of these aquariums, closely observe the behavior of the different sharks. How do the different species swim? Which fins do they use? How do they move their dorsal, caudal, anal, pectoral, and pelvic fins? What do they eat in captivity? How do they eat their food? What do they do when they're not feeding? Observing the sharks and answering these questions will help you to understand how perfectly these creatures are adapted to their environment.

Natural history museums, although they do not have live sharks, usually have excellent displays showing the different groups of sharks and illustrating their diversity. Visiting one of these displays is a good way to find out more about sharks. You can learn details about their behavior and the way they live and reproduce. Some big-city museums have excellent displays on sharks. They are the American Museum of Natural History, New York City; the National Museum of Natural History, Washington, D.C.; the Museum of Comparative Zoology, Harvard University, Boston, Massachusetts; the California Academy of Sciences, San Francisco, California; the Royal Ontario Museum, Ottawa, Canada; and the Los Angeles County Museum, Los Angeles, California.

If you become really interested in sharks, you may even want to keep one as a pet in your home. Numerous small sharks are available through pet shops, most notably horn sharks, nurse sharks, swell sharks, banded cat sharks, epaulette sharks, leopard sharks, and angel sharks.

Sharks are marine, so you will have to set up a saltwater aquarium. An all-glass tank is best, as the salt will corrode the metal parts of a metal-framed tank. The aquarium should be no smaller than 55-gallon capacity. Anything smaller will not comfortably house a shark.

You will need a large power filter outside the tank and an undergravel filter inside the tank. You must maintain a water temperature of 75° to 78°F. To do this you will need a thermometer in your tank. Often room temperature will keep the water at the proper temperature. If not you will need an aquarium heater.

Buy a synthetic ocean salt mix with which to prepare the water. Table salt will not work, because it is only sodium chloride. Seawater contains other salts in addition to sodium chloride, and it also has traces of various elements and minerals. Do not use seawater from a local beach. Inshore water is usually somewhat polluted, and its salt content is diluted by rivers and rainwater coming into the shallow water near the beach.

Feed your shark uncooked fresh or thawed fresh-frozen fish. Use only nonoily fish such as flounder, fluke, or halibut; not cod, mackerel, tuna, or bluefish, which are oily. You can also use shrimp. Most sharks will enjoy occasional treats, such as clams or crabs (shelled and raw) as well as squid. You should feed the shark no more often than every other day; often even every third day will do. Do not overfeed the shark. That will make it fat and cause it to pollute the tank water, which could cause the shark's death. Cut the food in strips and feed the shark as much as it will eat in ten minutes.

If you follow these guidelines, you should be able to enjoy your pet shark for many years. Most sharks become tame in captivity. Some will take food from your fingers (without biting you) and will allow you to pet them. Most nurse sharks like to have their bellies scratched.

Nurse sharks, leopard sharks, and angel sharks may eventually outgrow your home aquarium, but you will be able to keep them for several years because they grow quite slowly. Some species, like the horn sharks, epaulette sharks, and cat sharks, can also be bred in captivity fairly easily. Keep records of your pet shark: how much it grows, how often and how much it eats, and any interesting behavior it displays. Observe how it finds its food and eats, how it moves (which fins does it use?), and see when, where, and how it sleeps. The different species mentioned in the beginning of this section will do all these things in different ways. Keeping a pet shark is an excellent way to learn many fascinating details about sharks. When the shark becomes too large for your home aquarium you can either release it in the appropriate locale for its species or give it to a public aquarium.

Following are charts of shark locations.

ATLANTIC COAST, NOVA SCOTIA TO CAROLINAS

Species	Depth of Water	Seasons
Spiny dogfish shark	over 100 ft., midwater	spring, summer, fall
Greenland shark	over 100 ft., near bottom	winter
Atlantic angel shark	under 100 ft., on bottom	spring, summer, fall
Nurse shark	under 100 ft., on bottom	summer
Whale shark	over 100 ft., surface	summer
Sand tiger shark	under 100 ft., midwater	summer
Bigeye thresher shark	over 100 ft., surface	summer
Common thresher shark	over 100 ft., surface	summer
Porbeagle shark	over 100 ft., surface	all year
Mako shark	over 100 ft., surface	all year
Great white shark	over 100 ft., surface	summer
Basking shark	over 100 ft., surface	all year
Chain dogfish shark	over 100 ft., on bottom	all year
Smooth dogfish shark	under 100 ft., near bottom	spring, summer, fall
Blue shark	over 100 ft., surface	summer
Tiger shark	usually over 100 ft., midwater and surface	summer
Lemon shark	under 100 ft., surface	summer
Hammerhead sharks	over 100 ft., midwater	summer
Bull shark	all depths	summer
Atlantic sharpnose shark	over 100 ft., midwater	summer
Brown shark	under 100 ft., near bottom	summer
Dusky shark	under 100 ft., near bottom	summer
Silky shark	under 100 ft., surface	summer

ATLANTIC COAST, CAROLINAS TO FLORIDA KEYS

Species	Depth of Water	Season
Spiny dogfish shark	over 100 ft., midwater	winter
American sawshark	over 100 ft., on bottom	all year
Atlantic angel shark	under 100 ft., on bottom	all year
Nurse shark	under 100 ft., on bottom	all year
Whale shark	over 100 ft., surface	all year
Sand tiger shark	under 100 ft., midwater	all year
Bigeye thresher shark	over 100 ft., surface	all year
Common thresher shark	over 100 ft., surface	all year
Mako shark	over 100 ft., surface	all year
Great white shark	over 100 ft., surface	winter
Basking shark	over 100 ft., surface	winter
Chain dogfish shark	over 100 ft., on bottom	all year
Smooth dogfish shark	under 100 ft., near bottom	winter
Blue shark	over 100 ft., surface	all year
Tiger shark	all depths	all year
Hammerhead sharks	all depths	all year
Lemon shark	under 100 ft., midwater	all year
Bull shark	all depths	all year
Atlantic sharpnose shark	over 100 ft., midwater	all year
Brown shark	under 100 ft., near bottom	all year
Dusky shark	under 100 ft., near bottom	all year
Silky shark	under 100 ft., surface	all year
Blacktip shark	under 100 ft., surface	all year

GULF OF MEXICO COAST

Species	Depth of Water	Season
Nurse shark	under 100 ft., on bottom	all year
Whale shark	over 100 ft., surface	all year
Sand tiger shark	under 100 ft., midwater	all year
Bigeye thresher shark	over 100 ft., surface	all year
Common thresher shark	over 100 ft., surface	all year
Mako shark	over 100 ft., surface	all year
Chain dogfish shark	over 100 ft., on bottom	all year
Tiger shark	all depths	all year
Lemon shark	under 100 ft., midwater	all year
Bull shark	all depths	all year
Hammerhead sharks	all depths	all year
Atlantic sharpnose shark	over 100 ft., midwater	all year
Brown shark	under 100 ft., near bottom	all year
Dusky shark	under 100 ft., near bottom	all year
Silky shark	under 100 ft., surface	all year
Blacktip shark	under 100 ft., surface	all year

PACIFIC COAST, ALASKA TO NORTHERN CALIFORNIA

Species	Depth of Water	Season
Sixgill shark	all depths	all year
Sevengill shark	all depths	all year
Pacific spiny dogfish shark	over 100 ft., midwater	all year
Salmon shark	over 100 ft.	all year
Basking shark	over 100 ft., surface	spring, summer, fall
Great white shark	over 100 ft., surface	summer
Soupfin shark	over 100 ft., surface	summer

PACIFIC COAST, SOUTHERN CALIFORNIA TO MEXICO

Species	Depth of Water	Season
Frilled shark	over 100 ft., bottom, rare	all year
Horn shark	under 100 ft., bottom	all year
Prickly shark	over 50 ft.	all year
Basking shark	over 100 ft., surface	winter
Mako shark	over 100 ft., surface	all year
Great white shark	over 100 ft., surface	all year
Swell shark	under 100 ft., on bottom	all year
Gray smoothhound shark	under 100 ft., near bottom	all year
Brown smoothhound shark	under 100 ft., near bottom	all year
Leopard shark	under 100 ft., near bottom	all year
Soupfin shark	over 100 ft., surface	all year
Pacific angel shark	under 100 ft., on bottom	all year
Nurse shark	under 100 ft., on bottom	all year
Whale shark	over 100 ft., surface	all year
Common thresher shark	over 100 ft., surface	all year
Bull shark	all depths	all year
Lemon shark	all depths	all year
Blue shark	over 100 ft., surface	all year
Hammerhead sharks	all depths	all year

Sharks of the Atlantic
and Gulf Coasts

FAMILY SQUALIDAE: THE SPINY DOGFISH SHARKS

The spiny dogfish sharks make up a fairly large family of mostly small sharks, usually ranging up to about 4 feet in length. There are about eighty species in about twelve genera. This family includes the smallest species of shark, the dwarf shark, *Squaliolus laticaudus,* which is only 8 inches long. Spiny dogfish sharks are worldwide in distribution mostly in shallow waters, although some species live only at great depths. One member of this group, the Portuguese shark, has been caught at 9,000 feet—the greatest depth for any shark. All are live bearers, having up to about a dozen pups at a time. They prefer cold water, and in this family are the only species of sharks that live in Arctic and Antarctic waters.

The various species of the genus *Etmopterus* have light-producing organs on the sides of their bodies. Since they live at great depths where it is quite dark, some scientists believe that they use these light organs to attract prey.

The Atlantic Spiny Dogfish Shark

The Atlantic spiny dogfish shark, *Squalus acanthias,* is probably the most common shark in the North Atlantic. It reaches a maximum size of about 4 feet, although 3 feet is the average size. It can be identified by its silvery gray body covered with small white spots, two dorsal fins both preceded by a spine, and the absence of an anal fin. Dogfish sharks usually travel in schools of several hundred to many thousands of individuals. They are called dogfish because they travel and hunt in packs like dogs.

Tens of millions of pounds' worth of these sharks are caught every year. In England, the Atlantic spiny dogfish shark is commonly eaten in fish and chips. It is also used extensively as a dissection specimen in biology and comparative anatomy classes. Commercial fishermen dislike these sharks because if they catch a large school of them, the weight will cause the net to burst. What's more, the sharks bite through the nets.

Dogfish migrate extensively every year, following the cooler water temperatures. In winter they are found off Virginia and North Carolina. In spring they move northward, reaching Labrador and Newfoundland in midsummer. Although small, they live twenty-five to thirty years. Males do not mature until about ten years of age, and females mature at about twenty years. Gestation is about one year, with pups being born in midwinter off Virginia and North Carolina.

The spines preceding the dorsal fin of the dogfish are said to be venomous, causing inflammation and pain in humans. However, a fatality has never been reported as a result of this venom. Presumably the sharks use their venom as a defense against predators, mainly larger sharks. Dogfish feed on anything they encounter, mainly schools of small fishes and squid.

The Atlantic Spiny Dogfish Shark

The Greenland Shark

The Greenland shark, *Somniosus microcephalus,* is the largest member of the family *Squalidae,* reaching over 20 feet in length. It is the only species of shark that lives in the Arctic waters of the North Atlantic Ocean, and has even been found under the polar ice cap. It is very dark brown-black and can be identified by its large size, lack of an anal fin, relatively large eyes, and small dorsal fins that have no external spines preceding them. Because it is usually a slow, sluggish swimmer, it is often called the sleeper shark. However, large, active fish and even seals have been found in the stomachs of this species. This suggests that the Greenland shark can attain short bursts of speed to capture its prey.

In the summertime this shark is found only in deep, cold Arctic waters north of Newfoundland and Greenland. In the winter, as the water gets colder, it commonly comes south to shallow waters off Nova Scotia and the Gulf of Maine, and has been recorded off Massachusetts and Long Island. It is the only species of shark known to have flesh poisonous to human beings. It is not known what makes this fish poisonous, but boiling in several changes of water makes the flesh edible. It was once commonly caught, especially off Greenland for its liver oil, but the use of synthetic oils has lessened the demand. Its slow rate of growth, less than an inch a year, suggests an extremely long life span. It is ovoviviparous (live-bearing), producing about ten pups at a time.

The Greenland Shark

FAMILY PRISTIOPHORIDAE: THE SAWSHARKS

Sawsharks should not be confused with sawfish. The two can be easily distinguished, because the shark has long barbels (threads) under its snout and irregularly positioned "teeth" on its sawlike snout. These are not true teeth but, rather, enlarged, modified scales. Sawsharks are usually less than 5 feet long and are found mainly in the Indo-Pacific around Australia and Indonesia, where they are rather rare. There are five species in two genera, *Pristiophorus* and *Pliotrema*. They are live bearers, having less than a dozen pups at a time.

The American Sawshark

The American sawshark, *Pristiophorus schroederi,* is the only representative of this family found in the Atlantic Ocean. It can be readily identified by its sawlike rostrum, or snout, with long threadlike barbels underneath, and its large eyes. It can easily be distinguished from sawfish by the fact that its gill openings are on the sides whereas in sawfish they are on the bottom. Also, the sawshark has irregularly positioned rostral teeth, while these teeth are uniformly arranged in sawfish. Brown-gray in color, this species reaches only about 3 feet in length, including the saw. Found in water 500 to 1,000 feet deep, they have been caught only off the Bahamas and the east coast of Florida. Little is known about this unusual and interesting shark, and its range is probably larger than presently known.

American sawsharks sit on the ocean floor much of the time. They swim up into schools of fishes that pass overhead, using the "saw" to slash through the school, stunning and killing the fishes, which they then eat. Presumably the sawshark young are about 10 inches long at birth.

The American Sawshark

FAMILY SQUATINIDAE: ANGEL SHARKS

The angel shark family is made up of flat, almost raylike sharks. They grow to a length of 6 feet, and live mainly on the bottom in warm temperate seas worldwide. There are about twelve species in the one genus *Squatina.* All are ovoviviparous, bearing up to sixteen pups at a time.

The Atlantic Angel Shark

The Atlantic angel shark, *Squatina dumerili,* is common from Massachusetts to the Florida Keys and throughout the Caribbean and the Gulf of Mexico. It can be readily identified by its flat, skatelike body, which reaches close to 6 feet. The angel shark can be distinguished from skates and rays by the presence of free pectoral fin flaps, the front of which extend over the gill openings on its sides; in skates and rays the front of the pectoral fin is firmly attached to the side of the head, over the gill openings on the bottom side of the body.

The angel shark spends most of its time sitting on the ocean floor in shallow water. Camouflaged by its brownish color with black spots, it waits for a fish to swim close to it and then quickly darts out and grabs the fish with its long, slender teeth. Over long distances, it is a slow and sluggish swimmer. When caught, it is vicious, lunging and snapping at anything that moves. It will grab hold of something and hang on tenaciously like a bulldog. The young are about 10 inches in length at birth. Angel shark flesh is tasty and delicate, but it is rarely marketed as a food fish.

The Atlantic Angel Shark

FAMILY ORECTOLOBIDAE: NURSE AND CARPET SHARKS

Nurse and carpet sharks inhabit shallow inshore waters and normally lie on the bottom. They are rather stout, heavy-bodied sharks and can attain a length of 15 feet. Most species are found in tropical areas of the Indo-Pacific and the Red Sea. Some of these sharks are beautifully and colorfully marked, hence the name carpet sharks. There are about thirty species in twelve genera.

The Nurse Shark

The nurse shark, *Ginglymostoma cirratum,* is the only representative of this family in the Atlantic Ocean. It can be identified by the presence of a pair of barbels at the corners of the mouth, small eyes, and a small mouth under the head. Adults are a uniform brown while the young have numerous black spots on a somewhat lighter brown background. Reaching a maximum length of about 15 feet, they are about 12 inches long at birth.

A slow and awkward swimmer, the nurse shark spends most of its time sitting or crawling on the ocean floor. It can rotate its pectoral fins and use them to walk along the bottom. Its teeth are very short and stout to enable it to crush and grind up the shells of its prey, mainly crabs, shrimps, clams, and snails. Nurse sharks often congregate in groups in shallow water, lying in a pile of up to several dozen individuals. Mainly subtropical and tropical, they are common from the Carolinas to the Florida Keys and throughout the Caribbean and Gulf of Mexico to Brazil. In the summer they have been caught as far north as Long Island and Massachusetts.

Reproduction is ovoviviparous, with the eggs hatching inside the mother just before the pups are born. As many as thirty pups may be born at a time. They are hardy in captivity and have lived over twenty years in aquariums, where they become quite docile and can even be trained. Dr. Eugenie Clark, now at the University of Maryland, trained one to climb out of the water to receive its food. She later gave the shark to the emperor of Japan. The author, when he was at the New York Aquarium, had one nurse shark that enjoyed having its belly scratched.

The Nurse Shark

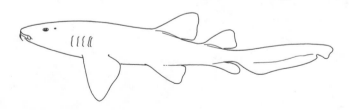

FAMILY RHINCODONTIDAE: THE WHALE SHARK

This family has only one known species, the whale shark, *Rhincodon typus*. It is the largest shark, and in fact is the largest living fish, reaching a length of 60 feet and a weight of 20 tons. It can readily be identified by its huge size, the distinctive white spots and stripes on a brown or reddish brown background, and its broad mouth. The mouth is filled with minute teeth, which are less than one-quarter inch in size in even the largest individuals.

Despite its size, it is harmless, living completely on plankton and small fishes, which it filters from the water. Internally the gill arches are modified into sievelike structures to sift the food from the water.

The whale shark is found worldwide in tropical and temperate waters. Along the Atlantic Coast of the United States it has been recorded as far north as Long Island. Slow and sluggish, it often swims at or near the surface. This has caused numerous whale sharks to be accidentally rammed by boats, usually causing more damage to the boat than to the fish. They usually swim alone, but they have occasionally been sighted in groups of up to a dozen individuals. The whale shark is docile, allowing divers to hitch rides sitting on its back or holding on to its dorsal fins.

Reproduction is ovoviviparous. The females hold the egg cases internally until the pups are ready to hatch from them. At birth, the pups are about 1½ feet long. Sixteen eggs were found in one female.

The Whale Shark

FAMILY ODONTASPIDAE: SAND TIGER SHARKS

The sand tiger shark family is a small one found worldwide in tropical and temperate seas. These sharks are often seen in aquariums as they are a hardy species in captivity. The sand tiger sharks attain a length of 15 feet.

The Sand Tiger Shark

The sand tiger shark, *Odontaspis taurus,* is often called the sand shark. This misleading name has been applied loosely to any fairly small shark found in shallow water. It has been used for smooth dogfish sharks, spiny dogfish sharks, and young sand tiger sharks, nurse sharks, and various requiem sharks.

The real sand tiger shark attains a length of about 10 feet, and is usually found in rather shallow water. The body is dark brown to bronze, often with some black spots on the sides. It can easily be identified by its two dorsal fins, which are about equal in size, its long, pointed snout, and the long, thin teeth that stick out from its mouth, giving it a toothy appearance. These teeth make the sand tiger shark a favorite for aquariums, as it looks ferocious. However, it is quite docile in captivity, as well as long-lived. The shark uses its long, thin teeth to catch and hold on to fishes, which make up virtually its entire diet and which it swallows whole. The teeth are not useful for biting things into pieces, nor are they used to bite chunks out of larger prey.

The sand tiger shark is common inshore along most of the Atlantic Coast and in the Gulf of Mexico. A rather sluggish swimmer, it is most active at night and sometimes sits motionless on the bottom in the daytime. This species has never been known to make unprovoked attacks on humans, but related species from South Africa and Australia have been aggressive toward humans.

Although they usually hunt alone, female sand tiger sharks will congregate to give birth in pupping grounds, which are often estuaries. At pupping time the females stop eating, presumably so that they will not eat their own young. Reproduction is ovoviviparous. The eggs are quite small, but as they develop in the mother's uterus, the young will eat one another to gain enough nourishment to grow. This in-uterine cannibalism occurs only in sand tiger sharks. As a result only two young are born at a time, one from each of the mother's two uteri. The young are about 3 feet long at birth.

The Sand Tiger Shark

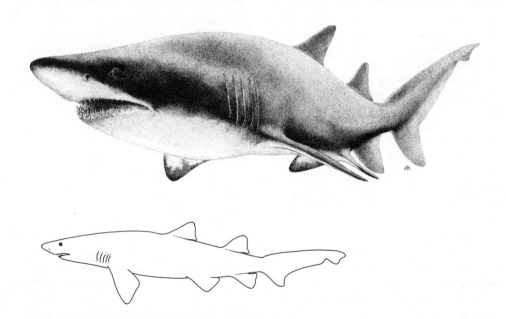

FAMILY ALOPIIDAE: FOX OR THRESHER SHARKS

The fox or thresher sharks are a small family, found in all temperate and tropical oceans. They are mostly oceanic, rarely seen near shore. They use their long tail (over half the body length) to thrash through schools of fish, stunning or killing them for food, hence the name thresher sharks. This behavior was first reported by fishermen and was considered a folktale until numerous scientists observed it. The maximum length of these sharks is about 20 feet. The flesh is tender and tasty, making these sharks highly sought after by fishermen. Thresher sharks have fairly small triangular teeth, which they use to bite pieces out of larger fishes and to grab hold of smaller fishes, which they swallow whole. Reproduction is ovoviviparous. The young are up to 5 feet long at birth, and so only two to four are born at a time. The mother continues to produce unfertile eggs while the young are developing, and the unborn pups eat these eggs for nourishment. This is called *in-uterine oviphagy*.

The Bigeye Thresher Shark

The bigeye thresher shark, *Alopias superciliosus,* can be identified by its large eyes, about one-quarter the size of the head, and a deep groove above the gill slits on each side of the head. Also, the gill slits are very large, almost touching on the shark's belly. Like all thresher sharks it has an enormously long tail. In total length this shark reaches about 20 feet. The shark's back is brownish or grayish, and the belly is creamy or silvery. It is found in water more than 100 feet deep off the Atlantic Coast from Maine to Florida, as well as in the Gulf of Mexico. In wintertime it moves farther south or out into deeper water. Only two young are born at a time.

The Common Thresher Shark

The common thresher shark, *Alopias vulpinus,* can be identified by its small eyes, less than one-quarter the size of the head, and by the lack of grooves above the gill slits. The back is dark brown to black, and the belly is white. It is more common than the bigeye thresher, to which it is similar, except that this shark usually gives birth to four or five young. It will reach 20 feet in length.

The Common Thresher Shark

FAMILY LAMNIDAE: MACKEREL SHARKS

This small family contains some of the best-known sharks, including the great white shark (discussed in Chapter 6) and some of the largest sharks. All mackerel sharks are fast, strong swimmers and can make spectacular leaps into the air. Scientists have suggested that they make these leaps to dislodge skin parasites. All have a half-moon-shaped caudal fin, as well as keels on both sides of their tail. Both the fins and the keels help to give them their speed and strength in swimming.

The Porbeagle Shark

The porbeagle shark, *Lamna nasus,* is the smallest of the mackerel sharks; the largest specimen recorded was 12 feet long, but porbeagles are rarely over 8 feet long. Blue-gray in color, this shark can be identified by four different characteristics: it has two lateral keels on each side of its tail; its first dorsal fin starts midway over the pectoral fin; its long, thin teeth have small lateral cusps; and it has no black spot in the axils of its pectoral fin. Common from Newfoundland to New Jersey in the past, it was heavily overfished during the 1960s by Europeans, who use it as a food fish, and it has been rather scarce since then. We can only hope that this species will recover. The porbeagle shark prefers cool, deep waters and feeds almost exclusively on other fishes. Its streamlined body makes it a fast swimmer, and this coupled with its long, thin teeth allow it to capture its prey easily. Reproduction is ovoviviparous, with the embryos being oviphagous in the uterus. Usually four young are born at a time in the spring.

The Mako Shark

The mako shark, *Isurus oxyrinchus,* is probably the most sought-after shark as a game fish. This is due to its spectacular leaps and tremendous fight when hooked as well as its delicious flesh. Mako steaks taste like swordfish and command a similar price.

Averaging 10 to 12 feet in length, makos have been recorded in excess of 18 feet. This shark is identified by several distinctive traits: the metallic blue of its back and the white of its belly; the single lateral keel on either side of its tail; a first dorsal fin that starts behind the pectoral fins; the absence of a black spot in the axils of the pectoral fins; and long, thin teeth with no lateral cusps.

Found from the Gulf of Maine to Florida and all through the Gulf of Mexico, the mako shark prefers warmer waters. It is found in shallower water in the summer, but it moves out into much deeper water in the winter. Off Long Island, New York, it is common about 20 miles offshore in water about 100 feet deep in the summertime. In the wintertime it migrates out to 100 miles or more offshore, where the depth is at least 1,000 feet and the water is warmed by the Gulf Stream.

The fastest shark, and probably the fastest fish, the mako has been recorded swimming at over 60 miles per hour. This, coupled with its extremely long, thin teeth, allows it to swim down and capture other fishes, its primary prey. It has been reported to have eaten tunas and swordfish, both of which are large. Under the skin along the side of the body, and especially in the tail, are dark red iron-rich muscles that give the mako the strength for this great swimming speed.

Reproduction is ovoviviparous, and the embryos are oviphagous. Ten to twelve pups are born at a time, and are about 2 feet long at birth. The fishing pressure on this beautiful and edible shark could lower its populations, as has happened with the porbeagle shark.

The Mako Shark

The Basking Shark

The basking shark, *Cetorhinus maximus,* is the second largest species of shark, next to the whale shark, and has been reported at close to 45 feet in length, although about 30 feet is the common length. The color is very dark, almost black. Sometimes classified in the family of Cetorhinidae, it is identified by its huge size, minute teeth, and very large gill slits, which almost meet under its head. The first dorsal fin starts far behind the pectoral fins. The basking shark ranges along the Atlantic Coast from Newfoundland to the Carolinas, rarely straying south to Florida, and is extremely rare in the Gulf of Mexico. It prefers cooler, deep waters. Like the huge whale shark, it is a filter feeder, sifting small organisms out of the water. To do this, it can open its mouth to huge proportions to take in water. Even in very large specimens the teeth are minute (less than one-fourth inch long in a 30-foot specimen the author dissected) and virtually useless. However, the skin is covered with large, sharp dermal denticles (skin teeth), which can cause severe lacerations. The water the basking shark takes in passes through the gills where there are modified dermal denticles that look and act like a comb to remove the food from the water.

The basking shark—so called because it often rests close to the surface as if basking in the sun—usually swims slowly, filtering the water as it goes along. However, it can put on great bursts of speed when it wants to, and like other lamnids it will make spectacular leaps out of the water. Usually docile like whale sharks, basking sharks will allow divers to approach them underwater and hitch rides on their backs.

A pregnant female has never been caught, but it is likely that they are ovoviviparous like other lamnids, and probably have two to four pups at a time, which are probably about 6 feet long at birth. They completely disappear in wintertime, and it is believed that they hibernate then, lying on the bottom in very deep water.

The Basking Shark

FAMILY SCYLIORHINIDAE: CAT SHARKS

There are about eighteen genera and eighty-seven species of cat sharks. Virtually all live in cold, deep water and are rarely caught. They get their names from their eyes, which are much like cats' eyes, elliptical with a thin slitlike pupil, usually brightly colored, either yellow or metallic green.

Many cat sharks are beautifully patterned or colored, and they are fairly small, usually under 4 feet in length. All are bottom dwellers, spending most of their time sitting on the ocean floor, where they eat crabs, clams, snails, and small fishes. Their bodies are stout, not streamlined for fast swimming. The teeth are short and rounded, designed for crushing the shells of their prey.

Cat sharks often have sensory barbels around the mouth to help them find their prey on the ocean floor. Some species are eaten for food, mainly in Europe.

The Chain Dogfish Shark

The chain dogfish shark, *Scyliorhinus retifer,* is one of the most beautiful sharks, having a chainlike pattern on its skin by which it is readily identified. A fairly small shark, reaching a maximum size of about 18 inches, it is quite common in cool water over 100 feet deep. Found from Maine to Florida and throughout the Gulf of Mexico, it is often caught by fishermen bottom-fishing in deeper waters. Its emerald green eyes are exceptionally striking. It is easily kept in aquariums, but needs cold water, about 50°F. Reproduction is oviparous; the eggs are light brown and about 2 inches long. Their leathery shell has tendrils at the ends that wrap around algae or rocks to help hold the eggs in place. The eggs are very common in certain places, suggesting that specific breeding areas exist. The young are about 4 inches long at hatching. Although several more species of cat sharks are found off the American coast, these are rare and live in very deep water.

The Chain Dogfish Shark

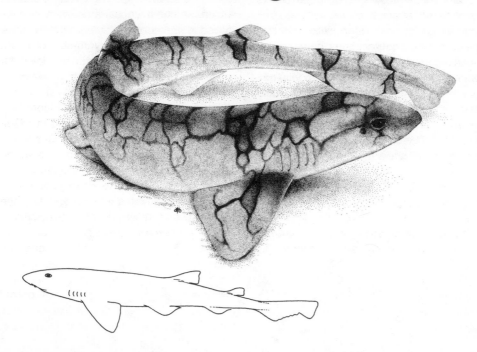

FAMILY TRIAKIDAE: SMOOTHHOUND SHARKS

The medium-sized smoothhound sharks are found in temperate and tropical seas worldwide. They are active swimmers that spend little time sitting on the bottom; they usually swim close to the bottom, however, where they catch most of their food. They eat mainly crustaceans and mollusks, only occasionally eating fishes, and their teeth are small and rounded for crushing their prey. Some Pacific Coast species such as the soupfin shark are eaten for food (see Chapter 5).

The Smooth Dogfish Shark

The smooth dogfish shark, *Mustelus canis,* is one of the most common sharks along the Atlantic Coast, probably second in abundance to the spiny dogfish shark. It can be identified by its small size, usually 3 to 4 feet, rarely 5 feet; short, rounded teeth; large spiracle (hole) behind the eye; rounded first dorsal fin; rounded lower lobe of the tail fin; and the rather broad, flat head. Its back is brownish or grayish, its belly is a paler color, and the edges of its dorsal fins are sometimes quite dark. It is common in water less than 50 feet deep from Maine to Florida and along the Gulf Coast. It migrates northward in summer and southward in winter. It is much more active at night than during the day. Reproduction is viviparous, with 10 to 20 pups born at a time, each one about a foot long. The flesh is tender and delicious and is usually sold under the name of grayfish.

The Smooth Dogfish Shark

FAMILY CARCHARHINIDAE: REQUIEM OR "TYPICAL" SHARKS

This is probably the largest family of sharks, with ten genera and over one hundred species. In body form and behavior they are what most people think of when someone mentions sharks. This group includes most of the species known to be dangerous to human beings. They are large sharks, some over 20 feet in length. Found worldwide in temperate and tropical seas, they are highly active and predatory. With their large, triangular, razor-sharp teeth, they can bite chunks out of large prey and grab hold of smaller prey, which they swallow whole. All species have a nictating membrane that serves as a thin eyelid to protect the eyes while they are grasping and struggling with prey.

Requiem sharks were once thought to swim continuously without ever stopping to rest, but Dr. Eugenie Clark of the University of Maryland has recently shown that numerous species do sleep on the floors of submarine caves off Mexico and Japan. This phenomenon probably occurs widely, and more research is needed to understand how they obtain oxygen while sleeping. Reproduction is viviparous in all species, with 30 to 50 pups in each litter.

The Blue Shark

The blue shark, *Prionace glauca,* is probably the most common requiem shark. It usually reaches 10 to 12 feet in length, and 20-foot individuals have been seen. It can be identified by its bright, metallic blue color; long, conical snout; long, sickle-shaped pectoral fins; finely serrated teeth, curving strongly backward in the upper jaw; and straight, narrow teeth in the lower jaw. The first dorsal fin is closer to the pelvic fins than to the pectoral fins.

This pelagic species rarely comes into water shallower than 100 feet. Ranging from Newfoundland to Florida along the Atlantic Coast, it has never been recorded in the Gulf of Mexico. It may migrate farther than any other shark. Individuals from off New England are known to have migrated as far away as the coasts of Brazil and Europe. These are the sharks that the New England whalers most dreaded, because blue sharks would flock in to feed on their kills.

The blue sharks' food consists mostly of fishes, but they will also feed on squid. Often they travel in groups, which will be all of one sex. Prolific reproducers, they are known to have litters of up to 130 young.

The Blue Shark

The Tiger Shark

The tiger shark, *Galeocerdo cuvieri,* is the largest requiem shark, commonly reaching 12 to 15 feet and recorded at over 18 feet in length. It is the most distinctive requiem shark, with dark gray to black spots or stripes on a gray to silvery background; a short, blunt snout; and uniquely curved, notched teeth.

The tiger is unquestionably one of the most dangerous sharks. As it swims through the water, it will swallow anything it encounters that will fit down its throat, hence its nickname, the garbage can shark. License plates and cans of paint have been found in tiger sharks' stomachs, not to mention parts of human bodies.

A most unusual incident occurred in April 1935. A 14½-foot tiger shark was caught off Maroubra Point, New South Wales, Australia, and brought alive to the Coogee Aquarium. Several days later it regurgitated its stomach contents, which included a human arm. Upon examination, it was found that the arm had not been bitten off by the shark, but rather had been cut off at the shoulder with a sharp instrument, probably a knife. Distinct tattoos on the arm and the fingerprints showed that the arm had come from a man who had been reported missing a week earlier. Police believed the man was murdered and cut into pieces that the murderer then threw into the ocean to hide all evidence. Although a suspect was arrested, he was never proved guilty because the arm was the only piece of evidence that a crime had been committed.

Common worldwide in tropical and temperate seas, the tiger shark is found from Massachusetts to Florida along the Atlantic Coast and all throughout the Gulf of Mexico. Considered a game fish, it puts up a strong fight when hooked, although it normally appears sluggish when swimming.

The Tiger Shark

The Lemon Shark

The lemon shark, *Negaprion brevirostris,* receives its name from the bronze to brassy color on its back, which changes to cream color on the belly. Usually averaging 8 to 10 feet, individuals have been recorded at over 12 feet in length. Besides its color, it can be identified by the second dorsal fin, which is as large as the first dorsal fin (in all other requiem sharks the second dorsal fin is distinctly smaller than the first dorsal fin), and its short, rounded snout.

The triangular teeth are finely serrated and slightly curved. It feeds mainly on other fishes, but will occasionally pick up mollusks and crustaceans from the ocean floor. The lemon shark easily becomes acclimated to captivity and thus is a favorite shark for public aquariums as well as for research purposes. It is a popular game fish and is commercially fished for its delectable flesh and strong skin, which is used to make expensive leather. Usually two to three dozen young are born at a time; these are about 18 inches long at birth.

The Lemon Shark

The Atlantic Sharpnose Shark

The Atlantic sharpnose shark, *Rhizoprionodon terraenovae,* is the smallest of the requiem sharks, averaging 2 to 3 feet and never longer than 4 feet. The back is brownish to grayish, often metallic, while the belly is white. It can be readily recognized by its small size, long conical snout, long grooves around the corners of the mouth, and triangular teeth curved inward with notches on their outer edges. The dorsal and caudal fins of the sharpnose shark are edged in black.

Usually common in shallow water, it often travels in schools, which are made up of individuals of the same size and sex. The Atlantic sharpnose shark is mostly found close to the bottom, where it feeds on mollusks, crustaceans, and small fishes. It is found from Maine to Florida and in the Gulf of Mexico and usually migrates north in the summer, and to the south and into deeper water in the winter. Not a favorite game fish due to its size, its flesh nonetheless is quite delicious. Less than a dozen young are born at a time; they are quite large in comparison to the size of the mother, being almost a foot long at birth.

The Atlantic Sharpnose Shark

The Bull Shark

The bull shark, *Carcharhinus leucas,* can be identified by its blunt, broad snout, a first dorsal fin that starts over the pectoral fins and is severely pointed at the tip, the lack of a ridge between the first dorsal fin and the second, and its broad, triangular teeth, which curve backward only slightly and have fine serrations on their edges. Averaging 6 to 10 feet, it has been recorded at 12 feet. Gray on the back, its belly is white. It is the only species of shark that will enter and remain in fresh water for long periods of time. It has been found several thousand miles from the ocean in Lake Nicaragua, the Zambezi River, and the Mississippi River. Originally these populations were thought never to enter the ocean, and thus to be distinct species in each of these freshwater areas. It is not certain why they enter rivers, but scientists believe that they may do so to rid themselves of skin parasites that cannot tolerate fresh water, or to exploit the rich freshwater food sources. Their skin in extremely thick and tough, and this may be an aid to them in their transition from salt to fresh water. The changes in salt concentrations require tremendous adjustments to maintain their internal water balance.

The bull shark is a voracious feeder, commonly feeding on other sharks as well as skates, rays, bony fishes, and anything edible that it encounters. It is therefore dangerous to humans, and numerous attacks have been recorded, in both salt and fresh water. Found from New York to Florida along the Atlantic Coast and throughout the Gulf of Mexico, it is most common around Florida and in the Gulf of Mexico, in shallow water. Although it usually hunts alone, females will congregate in large numbers in estuaries to give birth to their pups. When in these pupping grounds they do not feed, presumably so as not to eat their young and one another. The pups are about 2½ feet long at birth.

The Bull Shark

The Brown Shark

The brown shark, *Carcharhinus plumbeus,* averages 6 to 8 feet in length, occasionally reaching over 10 feet. It is often also called the sandbar shark, and is similar to the bull shark in having a short, blunt snout and a first dorsal fin that starts over the pectoral fins. It can be identified by these two characteristics combined with the distinct ridge on the back between the dorsal fins. The triangular teeth are strongly curved backward with fine serrations and are brownish to bronze on the inside.

Found from New England to Florida and throughout the Gulf of Mexico, it migrates north in summer and south in winter. Normally living in rather shallow water, it stays close to the bottom where it feeds on crustaceans, mollusks, and small fishes. A favorite sport fish, it has a delicious flavor. It often travels and hunts in small schools, and females congregate in large numbers in estuaries to pup. The pups, about 2 feet in length at birth, remain in the estuaries for several months before moving out to deeper water.

The Brown Shark

The Dusky Shark

The dusky shark, *Carcharhinus obscurus,* is a fairly large shark; it averages 8 to 10 feet and will reach over 12 feet in length. Its back is gray. It looks similar to the brown shark but can be distinguished by its first dorsal fin, which is pointed at the tip, and which originates behind the pectoral fins. The second dorsal fin's free margin is about the length of its base. Other characteristics are a ridge between the two fins on the back and triangular teeth curving backward with fine serrations on their edges. Usually solitary, the dusky shark does not appear to congregate in pupping areas to give birth. About a dozen 3-foot-long young are born at a time. Range, feeding behavior, and migration are like that of the brown shark, as is its desirability as a sport fish.

The Silky Shark

The silky shark, *Carcharhinus falciformis,* is similar to the brown shark and dusky shark. Averaging 7 to 8 feet in length, it reaches over 10 feet. The back is brownish or grayish. It is identifiable by its first dorsal fin, which has a rounded tip and begins close to the back of the pectoral fins. The second dorsal fin's free margin is considerably longer than its base. The triangular teeth curve backward slightly, are finely serrated at the tips, but are deeply notched close to their bases. Apparently rarer than the brown and dusky sharks, it is found from New York to Florida and the Gulf of Mexico. Migrating seasonally, it prefers shallow, warm water, where it feeds at the surface mainly on small fishes and squid. It is not actively sought as a sport fish, although it is edible.

The Blacktip Shark

The blacktip shark, *Carcharhinus limbatus,* is very distinctive: both dorsal fin tips, the caudal fin tips, and the pectoral fin tips are black while the rest of the fins and the back are metallic gray or sometimes bronze and the anal fin is pure white. Normally 5 to 6 feet in length, it sometimes reaches 10 feet. Found from New England to Florida and in the Gulf of Mexico, it is common around Georgia and Florida and along the northern Gulf Coast. The blacktip shark sometimes travels in schools; it feeds mainly on schooling small fishes and squid in shallow water. A fast, active shark, it also leaps out of the water. Because of this and its tasty flesh, it is a sport fish.

The Blacktip Shark

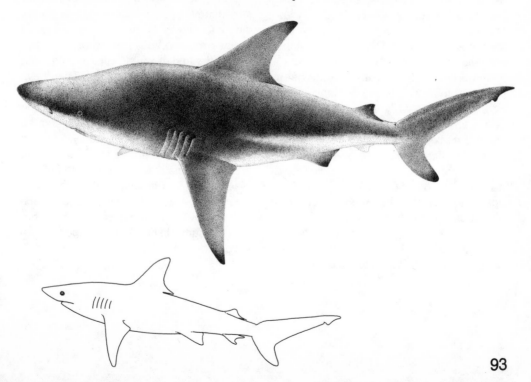

The Hammerhead Sharks

The genus *Sphyrna* contains about twelve species worldwide. These are called hammerhead sharks due to the broad lateral expansions of their heads, which are shaped like hammers. Their eyes are at the outermost points of the "hammerheads." Hammerhead sharks have often been placed in their own family of Sphyrnidae. However, anatomically they are typical requiem sharks except for the unique head shape that defines the genus. It has been suggested that their hammer-shaped heads help to streamline their bodies, or give them a better field of vision with the eyes wide apart; however, neither theory has been fully substantiated. Four species are found from New York to Florida on the Atlantic Coast and in the Gulf of Mexico: the bonnethead shark (*Sphyrna tiburo*), the great hammerhead shark (*S. mokarran*), the scalloped hammerhead (*S. lewini*), and the smooth hammerhead (*S. zygaena*). All four species look much the same, except for their head shapes, which easily identify the different species. Preferring warm water, all species migrate seasonally, north in summer and south in winter. All are highly active, feeding mainly on fishes. They have also engaged in numerous attacks on humans. Most are solitary, although some species form schools occasionally, and the bonnethead shark is commonly found in schools. The bonnethead shark is also the smallest species, averaging 4 to 6 feet and reaching 10 feet in length. The other species average 10 to 12 feet and will reach over 15 feet. The larger species are considered game fishes, and all species are sought for their edible flesh.

The Hammerhead Sharks

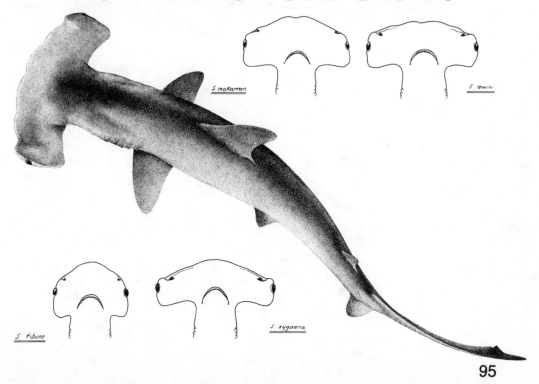

S. mokarran

S. lewini

S. tiburo

S. zygaena

95

Sharks of the
Pacific Coast

FAMILY CHLAMYDOSELACHIDAE: THE FRILLED SHARK

The frilled shark, *Chlamydoselachus anguineus,* is the only extant species of this primitive shark family whose fossil record goes back twelve to twenty million years. The frilled shark has unique trident-shaped primitive teeth and six pairs of gills, whereas most other sharks have only five. It receives its name from the large size of its gill flaps, which give it the appearance of having a frill around its head. It grows to a length of 6 feet and has a long, thin, eel-like body. Discovered off Japan in the Sagami Bay in the 1880s, it was long thought to live nowhere else. For unknown reasons, only in the Sagami Bay does it come into water as shallow as 100 feet. Recently it has been found at depths of 1,000 to 2,000 feet, and at these depths it seems to be widespread, as it has been caught off the coasts of Australia, South Africa, Europe, Chile, and southern California.

It feeds primarily on small fishes, which it swallows whole. Reproduction is ovoviviparous, with six to twelve pups per litter. It is rare off California, only known by two specimens, but it may be more common in deeper waters and more widespread. It is included here so that people will recognize it if they catch one and in the hope that they'll take it to a scientific institution so that we can learn more about this rare and unusual shark. It probably is also found off the Atlantic Coast, but in very deep water.

The Frilled Shark

FAMILY HEXANCHIDAE:SIX-GILLED AND SEVEN-GILLED SHARKS

This is another family of rather primitive sharks, having six or seven gill slits rather than the usual five. They are worldwide in distribution, mainly in deep seas. Their maximum length is about 20 feet. The upper-jaw teeth are long, thin, and straight, whereas the lower-jaw teeth are broad with numerous large, deep notches.

The Sixgill Shark

The sixgill shark, *Hexanchus griseus,* as its name tells us, has six pairs of gills and gill slits. It can be readily identified by these gill slits, along with only one dorsal fin, far back on the tail, beginning just slightly in front of the anal fin. Averaging 10 to 15 feet in length, it can reach 20 feet. Its back is gray to brown, its belly much lighter. Preferring cold water, it is usually found at depths greater than 500 feet, but especially at night it will come into much shallower water or even up to the surface to feed on fishes, squid, and crustaceans. Found from British Columbia to California, it has also been caught in the Atlantic Ocean and the Gulf of Mexico, but rarely and only in very deep water. Reproduction is ovoviviparous, with over a hundred 2-foot-long pups being born at a time. Apparently Puget Sound and San Francisco Bay are pupping grounds, and many young have been caught there.

The Sixgill Shark

The Sevengill Shark

The sevengill shark, *Notorynchus cepedianus,* can be identified by its seven sets of gills and gill openings, its gray to brown back with numerous black spots, a flat head with a broad, rounded snout, and one dorsal fin far back on the tail. It averages 5 to 7 feet in length; maximum length is 10 feet. Found from British Columbia to California, it appears to be more of a shallow-water species than the sixgill shark. Young are commonly caught in San Francisco, Tomales, and Monterey bays, all of which are on the California coast. Adults are rarely caught. This shark feeds exclusively on other fishes, apparently preferring other sharks, skates, and chimaeras. Reproduction is ovoviviparous, with up to eighty young being born at a time. Sevengill sharks are often kept in aquariums; however they rarely thrive in captivity. Their flesh is edible and is often sold in fish markets. Several provoked attacks on human beings have been reported.

The Sevengill Shark

FAMILY HETERODONTIDAE: HORN SHARKS

This small family of sharks has only six species, found in the temperate and tropical regions of the Pacific Ocean. Horn sharks grow to a length of 6 feet. They are easy to identify by their heavy brow ridges, which give them their name, and by a large spine preceding each dorsal fin. They are mainly bottom feeders, eating mollusks, crustaceans, and sea urchins. The teeth at the back of the mouth are large, broad, and rounded for crushing hard-shelled prey, whereas the teeth in the front of the mouth are small and pointed for grabbing prey. Hence their generic name *Heterodontus*: *hetero* meaning different, and *dontus* meaning tooth.

The Horn Shark

The horn shark, *Heterodontus francisci,* can be readily identified by its short, blunt head, with heavy brow ridges above the eyes, and spines preceding the dorsal fins. Averaging 3 feet in length, it rarely reaches over 4 feet. Its back is light gray or brown with black spots; the belly is cream. A bottom dweller, it spends virtually all its time sitting or crawling on the bottom and swims slowly and awkwardly. Clams, shrimps, and crabs are its most common food, but it will also eat small bottom-dwelling fishes. Usually found in water less than 20 feet deep, it is most active at night.

The horn shark is reported to migrate seasonally between deeper and shallower water. Reproduction is oviparous, and the egg cases are screw-shaped. The female takes these eggs in her mouth and wedges them between rocks. The eggs take about six months to hatch, and the young are 6 to 7 inches long at hatching. A favorite aquarium shark, it is hardy in captivity, living over ten years and even breeding in aquariums.

The Horn Shark

FAMILY SQUALIDAE: SPINY DOGFISH SHARKS

The Pacific Spiny Dogfish Shark

Some scientists think that the Pacific spiny dogfish shark, *Squalus suckleyi,* may be only a subspecies of the Atlantic form, *Squalus acanthias.* The Pacific species has fewer, larger white spots than the Atlantic species and sometimes no white spots at all.

Averaging about 3 feet in length, the Pacific spiny dogfish shark rarely exceeds 4 feet. It can be distinguished from other sharks by large spines preceding both dorsal fins, the lack of an anal fin, and a large eye and spiracle. It is found from the Bering Sea, off Alaska, to California. In other respects, it is like the Atlantic species, described above.

The Prickly Shark

The prickly shark, *Echinorhinus cookei,* is so named because of its large dermal denticles, which look like thorns, with a flat, star-shaped base and a long, pointed spine. This shark can be identified by these denticles, the lack of an anal fin, and the two small dorsal fins, which are not preceded by spines and are located far back on the short, stout tail. Average length is 8 to 10 feet, but specimens up to 15 feet long have been caught. The fins are usually edged in black, while the rest of the body is grayish brown. The prickly shark is usually found in water deeper than 50 to 60 feet, feeding on fishes close to the bottom; occasionally it comes to the surface. Reproduction is ovoviviparous with fifty to sixty 16-inch-long pups born at a time. Found off the coast of California, it is not caught frequently.

The Prickly Shark

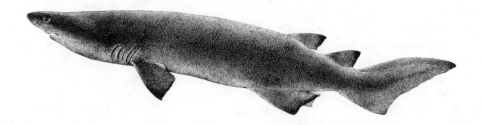

FAMILY LAMNIDAE: MACKEREL SHARKS

The Salmon Shark

The salmon shark, *Lamna ditropis,* receives its name from its tendency to follow and feed on schools of salmon. The first dorsal fin begins over the axil of the pectoral fin, and it has a lunate caudal fin and a strong keel on the sides of the tail continuing onto the caudal fin. Averaging 5 to 6 feet in length, it will grow to over 10 feet. Its back is dark blue-gray; the belly is white, with black spots on the sides and belly. The snout is short and conical, and the long, thin teeth have a small lateral cusp on each side. A pelagic, fast-swimming predator, it prefers cold water and migrates south in winter and north in summer. It is found from Alaska's Bering Sea to southern California. Besides salmon, it feeds on numerous other fishes as well as on squid. Especially during its migrations, it travels in schools of several dozen sharks. Reproduction is ovoviviparous, and two to four pups are born at a time. Like other lamnids, the female produces extra unfertilized eggs, which the embryos eat. Many fishermen dislike the salmon shark because it feeds on salmon; however it is an edible sport fish itself.

The Basking Shark

The basking shark, *Cetorhinus maximus,* is found from the Gulf of Alaska to southern California. See the discussion of the basking shark in Chapter 4.

The Mako Shark

The mako shark, *Isurus oxyrinchus,* is found in the Pacific from California south into the tropics. It is discussed in Chapter 4.

The Salmon Shark

FAMILY SCYLIORHINIDAE: CAT SHARKS

The Swell Shark

The swell shark, *Cephaloscyllium ventriosum,* is so named because it swallows water or air when attacked or frightened. This allows the shark to double the size of its abdomen, presumably to scare off the attacker by making the shark look bigger than it really is. About 3 feet long on the average, it will sometimes attain 4 feet. To identify the swell shark, look for a short, fat body, a flat, broad head with a wide mouth, and two dorsal fins on the tail. The first dorsal starts halfway over the pelvic fin; the second dorsal is directly over the anal fin. The body is medium brown with six to eight darker brown saddles and black spots. A sluggish swimmer, the swell shark spends most of its time sitting on the bottom where it feeds on small fishes. It prefers warm, shallow waters, and is found from central California southward. It is most active at night and is usually solitary. Reproduction is oviparous. The eggs are dark brown and take eight months to hatch the 6-inch-long pup. It is often exhibited in aquariums, but it isn't fished; its flesh is said to taste bad.

The Swell Shark

FAMILY TRIAKIDAE: SMOOTHHOUND SHARKS

The Gray Smoothhound Shark

Identify the gray smoothhound shark, *Mustelus californicus,* by its first dorsal fin, which begins behind the pectoral fins; its smooth, rounded teeth used for crushing its prey; and its gray color. Maximum size is about 4 feet. Found all along the coast of California, it prefers shallow water usually less than 20 feet deep. Living close to the bottom it feeds principally on crabs. Reproduction is viviparous with about a dozen 10-inch pups born in a litter. It usually swims in schools, often with leopard sharks. The gray smoothhound shark is edible and is often sold as a food fish.

The Brown Smoothhound Shark

The brown smoothhound shark, *Mustelus henlei,* can be identified by its first dorsal fin, which is farther forward than that of the gray smoothhound, starting over the axils of the pectoral fin. It averages about 2 feet in length and will reach about 3 feet. The teeth are sharp and pointed, and the body is brown. Common from Oregon southward, it prefers shallow waters near shore where it lives near the bottom and feeds on crustaceans and fishes. It is especially common in bays, such as San Francisco Bay, Monterey Bay, and the Gulf of California. Reproduction is viviparous, and the pups are 8 inches long at birth. Its flesh is edible, and it is sought after by fishermen.

The Brown Smoothhound Shark

The Leopard Shark

The leopard shark, *Triakis semifasciata,* is one of the most beautiful sharks, with its distinctive dark brown to black saddles and spots on a silvery gray background. Averaging 5 to 6 feet in length, the maximum length is about 7 feet. Found from Oregon to the Gulf of California, it lives in shallow water less than 30 feet deep. Traveling in schools that are often quite large, it eats mollusks, crustaceans, worms, and fishes on the bottom. Reproduction is ovoviviparous, with up to thirty pups per litter. The 8-inch pups are born in pupping grounds, which are usually bays such as San Francisco Bay. Hardy in captivity, it is a favorite shark for aquariums, where it will also breed. Individuals have lived over ten years in captivity. The flesh is also excellent, which makes it sought after by fishermen. It is a shy and wary shark in the wild as well as in captivity.

The Leopard Shark

The Soupfin Shark

The fins of the soupfin shark, *Galeorhinus zyopterus,* are used to make sharkfin soup; thus its name. Its second dorsal fin is located directly above the anal fin; the dorsal fins are equal in size. The lower lobe of the caudal fin is large, and there is a large spiracle behind the eye. Average size is 5 to 6 feet, with a maximum length of about 7 feet. The dorsal color is dark gray to black, and the belly is cream. Found from British Columbia to Baja California, it migrates north in summer, and south in winter. It is usually found in water 100 to 200 feet deep, and feeds between the bottom and the surface, eating all types of fishes as well as squid. Females will come into much shallower water to give birth to their pups. Reproduction is ovoviviparous, with up to fifty pups being born at a time; they're usually about 14 inches long. The soupfin shark is probably the most economically important shark on the West Coast, valued for its flesh, which is delicious, its fins, used for soup, and its liver, which is rich in vitamin A. Because of fishing pressure, the species was greatly depleted by the mid 1940s. We can hope the species will be able to make a complete recovery, but it has not yet done so.

The Soupfin Shark

FAMILY SQUATINIDAE: ANGEL SHARKS

The Pacific Angel Shark

The Pacific angel shark, *Squatina californica,* like its Atlantic relative can be distinguished from all other sharks on the West Coast by its flat body shape, similar to that of the skate. Averaging 3 feet in length, it can reach up to 5 feet. The anterior portion of the pectoral fins extends over the gills, which open laterally. The dorsal fins are small and far back on the tail. The teeth are long and thin. The back is light to medium brown, with many black spots; the belly is white. Found from southern Alaska to southern California, it spends almost all of its time sitting on the bottom, much like its Atlantic relative. It is usually found in water less than 50 feet deep, but occasionally it ventures into water several hundred feet deep. It feeds exclusively on fishes living close to the ocean floor. Reproduction is ovoviviparous, with a dozen or more young born at a time. It is most active at night. The flesh is edible, but it is not fished for.

ATLANTIC/PACIFIC SHARKS

Several species of sharks discussed in Chapter 4 are worldwide in distribution and are occasionally found along the southern California coast. These species are: the nurse shark, whale shark, common thresher shark, mako shark, bull shark, lemon shark, blue shark, and the hammerhead sharks. See Chapter 4 for information about these species.

The Great
White Shark

The great white shark, *Carcharodon carcharias,* is probably the best-known shark. It is also called the white pointer, man eater, white death, death shark, or just white shark. Because of its size, voracious appetite, and aggressive nature, it is an extremely dangerous and highly unpredictable shark. At times it is said to be wary and even shy of divers. However, it is a fast and determined attacker.

Although great white sharks can locate their prey by smell or pressure waves, they apparently rely most heavily on their vision. Once they have seen something interesting and have decided to attack, they charge their prey at speeds of 40 mph, propelled by strong side-to-side movements of their large half-moon-shaped tail. Their charge has been described as similar to an express train moving at full speed.

When they are several feet from their prey, they roll their coal black eyes back into their head, presumably to protect them from the wild thrashing of the attacked animal. While their eyes are closed, they use electroreception to home in on their prey. They align themselves for the attack by using their fins, which give the shark superb maneuverability. This, coupled with its cartilage skeleton, which gives it great flexibility, allows a shark to turn completely around within its own body length. As the shark grabs its victim, its jaws protrude out of its mouth, so that the razor-sharp teeth stick out in front of its nose. Even if the shark does not bite, the force of its charge is strong enough to knock a person backward several feet underwater.

When it bites its prey, the large jaw muscles thrust the hundreds of 2- to 3-inch teeth through the victim's body with a force of over a ton per square inch. Thus the teeth bite through skin, muscles, cartilage and bone with the ease of a surgeon's scalpel going through skin. Being able to take a 20- to 30-pound chunk of flesh out of its prey with every bite, it is easy to see why the great white is considered by many to be the supreme predator in the sea.

The great white is actually not white, but

The Great White Shark

rather slate gray or somewhat brownish on the back and cream on the belly. There is also a black spot on the side partially under each pectoral fin. This shark can also be identified by its large triangular teeth with deep serrations on the edges, a half-moon-shaped tail, pronounced ridges on the side of the tail, and coal black eyes. Averaging 15 feet in length, it can reach more than 20 feet. From the size of bite marks on seals and whales, it has been estimated that there are great white sharks over 25 feet in length. However, none of these monsters has been caught. Great white sharks about 20 feet long have weighed over 4,800 pounds.

The great white shark is found from Newfoundland to Florida on the Atlantic Coast, as well as in the Gulf of Mexico. On the Pacific Coast it has been recorded from southern Alaska to southern California. In the summer it is fairly common off Montauk Point, Long Island, on the Atlantic Coast, and between San Francisco and the Farallon Islands on the Pacific Coast. The great white shark migrates seasonally, not necessarily north and south, but rather offshore to deeper water in the wintertime. Even in the summertime the great white rarely comes into water shallower than 100 feet.

The great white has a reputation as a man eater. It has indeed made more known attacks on people than any other species of shark has. However, it is really not a man eater. It could more accurately be called a man biter! Recent studies of great whites, done mostly by Dr. John McCosker of Steinhart Aquarium in San Francisco, show that they feed mainly on sea mammals—whales, porpoises, and seals. Seen from below, a swimming person looks much like a sea mammal, with the arms and legs sticking out like the flippers of a seal or porpoise. The shark grabs this presumed seal from below, to eat it, but apparently great whites do not like the taste of human flesh, as they virtually always release the person after the first bite. Death may result from blood loss or organ damage caused by this bite, but rarely does the great white actually eat the person.

The attacks that great whites often make on boats are attributed to their electroreceptive sense. Metals in seawater, such as those on the hull or propeller of a boat, react with the salts in seawater to produce an electrical field similar to that given off by a living animal. It seems that the great white mistakes the electrical field of the boat's metal, and hence the boat, for a prey and attacks it.

Great whites prefer deep water, usually a hundred feet deep, or more. Thus the average swimmer is unlikely to encounter one of these sharks, as usually bathers are in less than 10 feet of water. The farther out you swim or dive, the more likely you are to encounter a great white shark, however. On the Atlantic Coast where there is a gently sloping continental shelf, you're not likely to encounter a great white until you are at least 10 to 15 miles offshore. On the Pacific Coast, however, the slope is much steeper, the water becomes much deeper closer to shore, and you could encounter a great white only a few hundred yards offshore. Seals appear to be a primary food source for great whites, and the seals' numbers are increasing now that they're protected under the Marine Mammal Act. As a result, the number of great whites is increasing somewhat also.

One of the most incredible attacks of a great white on a diver took place off Aldinga Beach, South Australia, where Rodney Fox was spearfishing in over 50 feet of water. Then, as he puts it: "It was a silence. A perceptible hush. Then something huge hit me on the left side with enormous force and surged me through the water. I knew at once what had happened—and was dazed with horror." The shark had virtually the whole left side of his chest in its mouth. With his rib cage crushed, stomach and lungs exposed, and his left arm torn open to the bone, he incredibly made it to the surface, where he was able to call to a nearby boat. He was rushed to a hospital, where he underwent four hours of surgery;

462 stitches were required to sew him up. In his own words he says, "I guess I just wasn't ready to go." His story also helps to show that great whites are more man biters than man eaters. Presumably the shark mistook him for a seal or porpoise. If you swim in areas where great whites are, try to find ways to look different from a seal so you won't be mistaken for one.

The great white shark has a countercurrent heat exchange system between its blood vessels, which allows it to keep its body temperature as much as 10°C above that of the surrounding water. In this countercurrent heat exchange system, the arteries running to the outside of the shark's body are next to the veins coming from the outside back to the center of the body. Thus, as the blood runs through the artery to the outside, it transfers its heat to the colder blood coming back in the vein. As a result the skin and outside parts of the shark's body are at the temperature of the surrounding water, but the center of the shark is warm and therefore can function more efficiently. It prefers cooler waters, and scientists believe that this countercurrent heat exchange system would cause its body to overheat if it lived in warmer water.

Little is known about the reproduction of great white sharks. A pregnant female has never been caught and recorded. A questionable report from the Mediterranean early in the 1900s reported a female great white with nine embryos, each 2 feet long and weighing 108 pounds apiece. Since free-swimming great whites have been caught, which were only about 5 feet long and weighed only 50 to 60 pounds, this report is highly suspect. Presumably the great white is like other lamnid sharks and bears only a few young, which feed on unfertilized eggs, produced by the mother in the uterus. Probably great white pups are born at about 3 feet in length. Although pupping grounds are not precisely known, it seems likely that the waters off Montauk Point, Long Island, are a pupping ground.

Considered a game fish, the great white shark is avidly pursued by sport fishermen.

Its flesh is delicious, and the teeth are used to make jewelry. Hence it is also sought by commercial fishermen.

Especially since the movie *Jaws,* the great white shark, like other sharks, has been the target of many shark tournaments. The intent of these tournaments is to wipe out this "dreaded killer." However, we should remember that when we go into, or on, the ocean, we are invading the shark's territory. The shark was born there, grew up there, and the great white has spent over 30 million years evolving there.

When a great white shark attacks a person, it is only following its instincts in obtaining food for itself. It does not have a malicious intention of destroying every human being on earth. Why, then, should people want to maliciously kill every great white shark just for the sake of killing it? We should strive to find ways to avoid or prevent great white attacks. In this way humans and great whites could co-exist in the sea without threatening one another. The populations of great white sharks, as well as other sharks, have declined in certain areas because of shark tournaments. Perhaps we can learn to appreciate the beauty and elegance of the great white and its value in its natural environment. We must ensure that it does not become another vanished species, and we must learn to share the ocean with the great white shark so that it can maintain its proper position in nature.

The Shark's Ancestors

Sharks evolved about 300 million years ago—before the dinosaurs appeared—during the Devonian Period. They probably evolved from a placodermlike ancestor, although some scientists believe they may have evolved from acanthodians. Both of these are now extinct groups of fishes that look externally somewhat like sharks. Both grew to fairly large sizes, some to about 20 feet. The placoderms had much of their body covered with scaleless skin, but their head was covered with large, hard plates. Their teeth were fused together into tooth plates, which look much like a turtle's beak. They had a cartilage skeleton, similar to today's sharks. Acanthodians' skin was covered with small, scalelike structures. Their teeth were small and conical, much more like a bony fish's teeth. Although much of their skeleton was made up of cartilage, there was one major difference: they also had some true bones. More detailed studies need to be done before we know for sure from which group sharks arose.

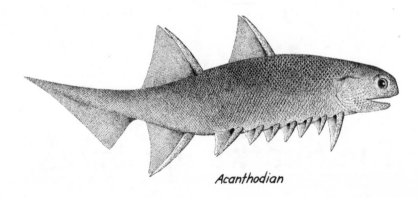

Acanthodian

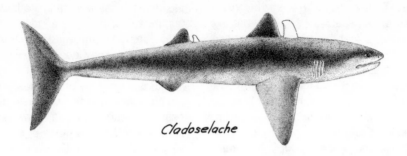

Cladoselache

During those hundreds of millions of years, sharks have changed little in external body form and function. One of the earliest known sharks, *Cladoselache,* looks much like today's sharks. Only if we examine the insides can we see how primitive it is. As today's sharks evolved, they made many special adaptations to their habitat. From *Cladoselache* the early sharks produced no less than twelve groups of fossil sharks. To give you an idea of their diversity, all living sharks today are placed in the one group of *Neoselachii,* meaning "new sharks." The twelve groups of fossil sharks have greater differences from one to another than living sharks do, greater even than the difference between the large predaceous great white and the small bottom-dwelling angel shark. Of course, in the fossil groups many of the differences were internal, rather than on the outside. There were different types of teeth, different kinds of spines on different parts of their bodies. In some the shape and placement of the fins were very different from those in living sharks. Today there are about three hundred extant species of sharks, but experts estimate that there were at least two to three *thousand* species of fossil sharks. From the fossils we can see that sharks did a lot of changing during their evolution over the last 300 million years. All animal groups change drastically during their evolution; you know that the reptiles produced the dinosaurs as one of their groups, for example.

Basically, all the shark groups maintained their streamlined, torpedo-shaped body. This shape allowed them to move through the water easily and rapidly, and was carried on to today's sharks. Internally, however, especially in their skeleton and in the detailed structure of their teeth and dermal denticles, sharks have changed drastically. The shark's development is an example of conservative evolution, wherein the general body form is conserved, but the underlying body parts have changed and been vastly improved. This overall body shape has probably been conserved so well because, for fast-swimming predators in the sea, the shark's body is an ideal form, perfectly adapted to the sharks' way of life.

Most of our knowledge of extinct sharks comes from our study of fossil teeth. Since sharks do not have any bones, the teeth and fin spines are the parts that most often fossilized easily and well. However, occasionally a rare find is made of the cartilage skeleton of one of these extinct forms preserved intact. Such rarities show us how similar in design living sharks are to the fossil ones from millions of years ago.

The Bear Gulch formation in Montana is one of the localities where whole fossil sharks are found. It may seem surprising that fossil sharks would be found in an inland area like Montana. However, about 150 million years ago, when this formation was produced, the ocean levels were much higher than they are today because there weren't any polar ice caps. As a result, the whole central part of the United States (roughly the entire Mississippi River basin) was an extension of the sea. The water was relatively shallow—probably less than 50 feet—and warm. It supported a rich marine fauna of fishes and invertebrates. Today the formation is exposed on the surface in an area covering several acres. Underground it probably continues for hundreds, or even thousands, of miles. Dr. Richard Lund of Adelphi University is carrying on studies of the Bear Gulch formation, increasing our knowledge of these early fossil forms.

Some of the most unusual fossils are the teeth of the extinct great white shark, *Carcharodon megalodon.* Some of the teeth

Reconstruction of the jaws of Carcharodon megalodon

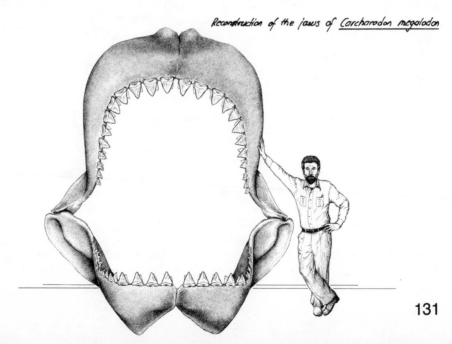

that have been found are up to 10 inches long, hence the name *megalodon,* which literally means "big teeth." These teeth are approximately 10 to 30 million years old and are commonly found in shell marls of Florida, Georgia, and the Carolinas. The sharks they came from have been estimated to be up to 60 feet long.

Sharks and People

The one characteristic for which sharks are probably best known is their capacity to kill and eat humans. Actually less than one-tenth of all shark species have been implicated in unprovoked shark attacks. We will only consider unprovoked attacks here, as any animal will protect itself if provoked or molested, even a pet dog or cat.

There are several factors to consider in shark attacks. First off, when we enter water, we are leaving our domain—land—and entering the sharks' domain—water. Human beings are clumsy in water, whereas sharks are swift, lithe, and elegant; they are perfectly adapted to their environment. Many people think of the ocean as being full of bloodthirsty, life-threatening sharks. This could not be further from the truth. Remember that thousands more people are killed by other people than by sharks every year; thousands more people are killed in automobile accidents than by sharks every year; and more people are even killed by lightning every year than by sharks. Human beings kill tens of thou-sands of sharks every year; many do so just so they can hang a trophy on a wall. And yet there are less than a hundred shark attacks on human beings every year, and few of them are fatal.

As we have seen, the great white shark has the greatest reputation for attacking people. Other species of sharks, mostly carcharhinids, attack for the purpose of feeding. Most dangerous are the tiger shark and various species of hammerhead sharks. Large individuals of these species are able to eat a whole person; smaller sharks would only take bites out of a person. Besides the large carcharhinids, the only other species that is a confirmed man eater is the Australian sand tiger shark. Sharks do not acquire a taste for human flesh, but if one of these sharks is hungry and a person is in the water, the shark will eat the person just as readily as anything else.

Much research has gone into how to prevent shark attacks. Various chemicals, air bubbles, and electric fields have been tried to deter attacks. Some are useless, and others will deter some species of sharks, but actually attract others! Dr. Eugenie Clark has been experimenting with a skin secretion produced by the Moses sole, a fish found in the Red Sea. This chemical may deter attacks by all species of sharks.

Here, again, is some general advice on how to avoid shark attacks:

1. Do not swim where large sharks are common.
2. Do not swim in an area where a shark has been seen recently.
3. Do not swim at dusk or at night.
4. Do not swim alone.
5. Do not swim if you are bleeding or have any open wounds.
6. Do not thrash around or splash in the water, as this attracts sharks, but rather swim smooth and evenly.
7. Stay in shallow water, as the larger sharks prefer deeper water.
8. Do not molest or provoke a shark, whatever its size.

People use sharks in many ways. Sharks are eaten as food in many parts of the world. Shark skin, because of its dermal denticles, was widely used as shagreen—a substitute for sandpaper—in the fine finishing of furniture. The skin, tanned and with the dermal denticles removed, is a durable leather that commands a high price in America, Europe, and Russia. It is often used for shoes, wallets, and handbags.

The oil from sharks' livers is rich in vitamin A. Until synthetic substitutes were found, shark liver oil was commonly used as a substitute for cod liver oil. The liver from a 15-foot shark can yield as much as 18 gallons of oil.

The teeth of sharks are in high demand for jewelry-making, and are used in necklaces, bracelets, and rings. In Australia a set of great white sharks' jaws (from which the teeth are sought for jewelry) will bring in as much money as two tons of tuna—about $1,000. Sharks' jaws are also in high demand as decorations and trophies.

To provide sharks for commercial uses

there were, and still are, numerous shark fisheries off the coasts of Australia, South Africa, England, Japan, and the United States. In many areas sharks are also favorites among sport fishermen. The mako shark is considered one of the best sport fish because it will put up a great fight. It is one of the fastest-swimming sharks, and when hooked it will make spectacular leaps out of the water.

Many scientists around the world are studying sharks to learn more about their biology, which is still relatively little known. Astonishing new facts are being learned about sharks every year. One of the most recent discoveries is that sharks almost never get cancers because they produce a chemical in their bodies that is carried through the entire body by the blood. Apparently when cells in the body become cancerous, this chemical specifically kills these cells, thus stopping the cancer. It is hoped this chemical will be useful in treating human cancers.

Sharks can also orient themselves by geomagnetic fields—just as we use a compass. Through tag-and-recapture studies, researchers have learned that some sharks migrate over 3,000 miles every year. The National Marine Fisheries Service has run a shark-tagging program for over twenty years, now supervised by Jack Casey. This is probably the largest shark-tagging program in the world. To date over 45,000 sharks have been tagged. One shark was recovered seventeen years after it was tagged. From this research, it appears that the blue shark probably migrates farthest. Some tagged off Long Island, New York, have been recaptured off Europe, West Africa, and Brazil.

As scientists continue to study these fascinating animals, they will certainly discover many more facts about sharks. That expanding knowledge should lead us to realize what beautiful and fascinating animals sharks are and strive to preserve them and share the oceans with them.

Glossary

Anal—Referring to the fin on the underside of the tail.

Anterior—Toward the front or head.

Caudal—Toward the tail; also refers to the tail fin itself.

Dorsal—Toward or on the back.

Lateral—Toward or on the sides.

Oviparous—A mode of reproduction in which eggs are laid outside the mother's body.

Oviphagous—A form of embryonic feeding in which the embryos in the mother feed on unfertilized eggs.

Ovoviviparous—A mode of reproduction in which the mother carries the eggs internally until they are ready to hatch.

Pectoral—Referring to the large paired fins on the sides of a shark close to the head.

Pelagic—Living far out in the open ocean and never coming close inshore.

Pelvic—Referring to the paired fins on the belly of a shark, about midway on the body.

Posterior—Toward the tail.

Rostrum—Projecting nose or snout.

Ventral—Toward or on the belly.

Viviparous—A mode of reproduction in which the young are carried in the uterus of the mother, often with a placentalike connection.

Bibliography

Baldridge, H. David. *Shark Attack.* New York: Berkley Medallion Books, 1974.

Bigelow, Henry, and William Schroeder. *Fishes of The Western North Atlantic,* Part 1: Sharks. New Haven: Sears Foundation for Marine Research, Yale University, 1948.

Budker, Paul. *The Life of Sharks.* New York: Columbia University Press, 1971.

Castro, José. *The Sharks of North American Waters.* College Station: Texas A & M University Press, 1983.

Ellis, Richard. *The Book of Sharks.* New York: Grosset & Dunlap, 1975.

Gilbert, Perry W., ed. *Sharks and Survival.* Boston: Heath, 1963.

Gilbert, P. W., R. F. Mathewson, and D. P. Rall, eds. *Sharks, Skates, and Rays.* Baltimore: Johns Hopkins University Press, 1967.

Lineaweaver, Thomas H., III, and Richard H. Backus. *The Natural History of Sharks.* Philadelphia: Lippincott, 1969.

McCormick, H. W., T. Allen, and W. Young. *Shadows in the Sea: Sharks, Skates, and Rays.* Philadelphia: Chilton, 1963.

Index

About the Author

Guido Dingerkus received his B.S. and M.S. degrees from Cornell University and his M.Phil. and Ph.D. degrees from City University of New York. He has studied and collected fishes, and especially sharks, extensively on the Atlantic, Pacific, and Gulf of Mexico coasts of North America and Central America, as well as in Europe. He has published numerous scientific papers on sharks and other fishes. While curator of the New York Aquarium, Dr. Dingerkus set up the aquarium's shark exhibit, collected specimens for it, and routinely hand-fed the sharks underwater. Presently he is Field Associate of the Department of Ichthyology at the American Museum of Natural History in New York City.

About the Artist

Dietrich L. Bürkel is an avid fisherman, scuba diver, photographer, and illustrator who has caught, studied, and drawn fishes for many years. Especially interested in sharks, he holds several shark rod and reel records, and is presently the official recorder for the International Game Fish Association in Germany. He has illustrated several books on fishes and fishing. Formerly Keeper of Natural History at the Glasgow Museum, Scotland, he is presently Keeper of the Public Display Museum at the University of Hamburg, Federal Republic of Germany.